The
British Submarine
Service

THE E CLASS SUBMARINE

The
British Submarine
Service

The Royal Navy & the
submersible war 1914-1918

"Klaxon"

John Graham Bower

LEONAUR

The
British Submarine
Service
The Royal Navy & the
submersible war 1914-1918
by "Klaxon"
John Graham Bower

First published under the title
The Story of our Submarines

Leonaur is an imprint
of Oakpast Ltd

ISBN: 978-1-84677-972-5 (hardcover)
ISBN: 978-1-84677-971-8 (softcover)

http://www.leonaur.com

Publisher's Notes

In the interests of authenticity, the spellings, grammar and place names
used have been retained from the original editions.

The opinions of the authors represent a view of events in which he
was a participant related from his own perspective,
as such the text is relevant as an historical document.

The views expressed in this book are not necessarily
those of the publisher.

Contents

CHAPTER 1

A Retrospective View: 1918

1

There has naturally been a great deal of ink spilled during the War on the subject of the U-boat. The British Submarines have worked unseen and unheard of. Occasionally a few official lines have appeared in the newspapers about them, but the very nature of the work they have been doing has precluded any divulging of their activity. With the permission of the Admiralty I am about to speak now of some of the work they have done, and to give their own reports describing some of the many occasions on which they have been in contact with the enemy.

On August 4, 1914, we had in our Submarine Service the following boats: 9 E class, 8 D class, 37 C class, 10 B class.

Of these, the B and C classes were 320 tons submerged displacement, and were not suitable for the patrol round the mouth of the Bight. The D and E boats were designed for that purpose, being of 600 and 800 tons submerged displacement respectively. The B and C classes were used in the War for local patrols, defence of the coasts and ports, and (as the War progressed and they became obsolete), for instruction of new entries of personnel.

Before I get on to the War itself I want to give a short description of the entry and training of our personnel both before and after the War began.

In peace time an officer who wished to join the Submarine Service had first to receive a recommendation from his own captain. He then had to produce either a first-class certificate for his Torpedo examination for lieutenant, or, if he had not that qualification, a certificate from the torpedo-lieutenant of his ship to the effect that he showed special zeal in that branch of his duties. If his name was accepted it was placed at the bottom, of the candidates' list, and in due time, after an interval which varied from year to year, he was appointed to Fort Blockhouse, the Submarine Depot at Gosport. There the batch of new officers were medically examined, and (the standard being high) the unfit were weeded out and returned to their ships.

For the next three months he went through a course of practical submarine instruction, his training period terminating in examinations which provided another obstacle, the meshes of which prevented certain candidates from proceeding further.

The officers of the class were then sent as "third hands" to different boats to await vacancies as first lieutenants. After two to four years as first lieutenant (the time varied with the number of new boats built), an officer obtained command of an A boat (of 204 tons), from which he rose by seniority to larger and more powerful commands.

The men entered in much the same way, being recommended, of first-class character and of excellent physical standard. They went through a less comprehensive training course, but had the same weeding-out to undergo, so that as far as possible the "duds" were got rid of before they had cost the country much in useless teaching.

In war-time it has not been possible to spare the time for the full instructional courses, but the courses continued, although much shortened. The shortage of personnel in the Navy generally cut down the field from which volunteers were drawn, but in spite of this the Submarine Service was able to keep up its voluntary entry, and to continue to retain its standard by drafting back those who were by nature or capabilities unfit for such work. The submarine sailor is a picked man, and is the admiration of his officers. There is a Democracy of Things Real in the boats which is a very fine kind of Democracy. Both men

8

and officers in a submarine know that each man's life is held in the hand of any one of them, who by carelessness or ignorance may make their ship into a common coffin; all ranks live close together, and when the occasion arises go to their deaths in the same way. The Fear of Death is a great leveller, and in submarines an officer or a man's competency for his job is the only real standard by which he is judged.

In the German Navy, before the War, the Submarine Service had not received the attention it might have done. There, the submarine officer did not hold the status in the eyes of his Navy that was held by his destroyer or battleship brother. Since the accident to U-3 at exercise practice, also, certain rules for exercise had been introduced, which precluded practice attacks on target-ships going at high speed, and had circumscribed the areas (by defining "safe" depths of water) in which exercises might be carried out. In our Navy it had always been recognised that risks must be incurred in peace, so as to ensure greater safety in war. As far back as 1912 our submarines were practising attacks on destroyers zigzagging at high speed, and were diving in any waters, and generally reproducing war conditions as far as possible. While even in 1904 the early boats on manoeuvres were allowed to dive under surface ships, and destroyers were allowed to use wire-sweeps against them.

For years before the War a Submarine Defence Committee of officers was working to find the best antidote to the submarine menace, and experiments were carried out by the Committee with our own boats. The result of this was that, on the War coming, both the submarine officers and those of our Navy whose task it was to deal with the U-boat had considerable experience to begin on.

The British Submarine Flotillas, as shown in the preceding list, comprised in 1914 far more small boats than sea-going ones. This was altered later as the strategy of the War crystallised, but when the War began it had never been expected that the enemy Fleet would remain so inactive. The Navy's view had naturally been that the German had not built such a fine Fleet if he wasn't going to use it, and so the majority of our boats, instead of being designed for "Over There" work, were designed for "half-way over." And very good boats the C boats were, too. If the expected War of Movement had taken place, with a North Sea dotted with racing cruisers, and ships of both sides looking for a fight, every boat in our service would have been in the thick of the trouble. As it was, the course of events very soon showed that the ring round the Heligoland Bight—the blockading patrol—was to be the chief station of our submarines in Home waters.

Both belligerents began to design and build at once. The German went straight ahead on the one type, which, with variations, has served him throughout the War—*viz.*, the commerce-destroying medium-sized patrol boat. To this type he later added the mine-laying submarine, and towards the end of the War he evolved the large commerce-destroying cruiser boat.

New, both before and during the War, we held a lead over our enemy in the matter of submarine design. That statement is confirmed by the data given by the U-boats arriving at Harwich as I write. Some time ago the British Navy prepared an antidote to a design of submarine which it was thought the enemy must, by logical reasoning, soon produce as being the obvious thing for him to think of. Our antidote has not yet had a chance to be used, as it was only recently that the German designers got to that stage in their reasoning.

But what did we build? Well, we did not want commerce destroyers at least; such work as the cutting of the Turkish communications in the Sea of Marmora and the sinking of transports in the Baltic could be done by our ordinary E boats. But we did want mine-layers, and we built those. What else? Well, I must branch off into a dissertation on submarines generally.

A submarine may be any kind of surface vessel, with the advantage added to her of being able to dive. She need not necessarily be a diving boat with a few torpedo tubes and a couple of guns. She may be anything. A surface ship can only be one thing; you cannot have a cruiser-monitor or a destroyer-battleship. But a submarine may be two things at once; and a submarine can, as a result, act unsupported. Take the case of a scouting submarine. What is the alternative? If we had no scouting submarines we would have had to keep a ring of destroyers out to watch the Bight.

Those destroyers might, being out near the enemy's coast, be attacked by enemy cruisers, so that it would be essential to keep our cruisers out in support. Then if the enemy brought out—and so on—up to the final result of our battle fleet being continuously at sea, which would have been not only unnecessary wear and tear on the big ships, but a good opportunity for the U-boats if they had cared to take a chance. Take the case of the submarine mine-layer. She has the great advantage, to begin with, of not only getting to her position unseen, but of being able to lay her unpleasant cargo down unsuspected and unobserved.

Then, again, she does not need a supporting force to follow her in case she meets with trouble. She does not look on a big enemy ship as a trouble, should one interfere with her; she would rather describe the big ship as a "gift." She is open to the usual anti-submarine methods, and can be dealt with by destroyers, seaplanes, and so on; but if she succumbs to their attacks—well, that is another submarine gone, but it might have been a big surface ship.

By the nature of the German strategy our lines of design were indicated. The chief type we needed were scouts—in other words, patrol boats. We built these in considerable numbers, for the several types of patrol boats we diverged into were capable of doing any of several things. They could do the Heligoland Bight patrol, attacking the enemy if met with, and reporting to the C.-in-C. what they saw on their patrols; they could go out into the Atlantic to hunt U-boats on the traffic lanes, or they could go to the Mediterranean to work in the Adriatic. They were the general-utility craft of the Submarine Navy.

The mine-layers were of the patrol boat type, getting larger as the War went on, but always with the torpedo-tubes (reduced in number) built into them to allow them to become normal

11

submarines when a chance arose.

In the early part of the War there were some additions to the Submarine Flotillas in the shape of V-W and F boats of 500 submerged tonnage. These were experiments by the Admiralty in building boats of foreign design, drawings being used of the Laurenti and Fiat firms. After these boats had been tried and their best points copied into our own designs, the standard British ideas were reverted to for war construction. The building of these boats served its purpose in giving us an insight into the lines upon which other nations were working, but foreign designs were not continued owing to the better performances of our own boats.

The G and J class were patrol boats—the G's being of 975 ton submerged displacement, and so larger and with more beam than the E boats; the J's were 19-knot boats of 1820 tons submerged, and marked a great advance in the big-submarine type. The year 1915 gave us the addition of a number of E class, while the G's began to join up with the Flotillas in November of that year. The first J boat commissioned in the spring of 1916.

The H class were small patrol boats of American design—a design later enlarged and improved in England. The L boats were enlarged and improved E's, and are probably the finest patrol submarines in existence.

The 4th August 1916 saw the commissioning of a boat which was a revolution in submarine design. This was the first K boat. This class was designed for the expected Fleet action; their qualities were to be—that they should have several knots in hand over the speed of the Battle Fleet, that they should be seaworthy and able to cruise with the Fleet, and that they should have the necessary submarine qualities to enable them to deal with the High Sea Fleet when it should be met.

These qualities they have; but it is regretted that the enemy gave them no chance of trying their luck in action. They were used on patrol to keep them from getting stale during the long wait for their "Day," and their experiences on patrol, and when at sea on the periodic occasions when the Fleet went hurrying out in reply to reported enemy activity, have given invaluable data for future construction of large and fast submarines. These boats are of 1880 tons (surface) and 2550 tons (submerged) displacement. They have a speed of slightly over 24 knots on the surface, can carry a good gun battery if required, and their hulls being low and well stream-lined, and their torpedo armament powerful, they can act both as destroyers by night or as submarines by day.

These boats have a battery capacity sufficient for a day's Fleet battle, but no more. They may be described as having great strategic speed and capacity, but small tactical radius: that is, they can get to the place where they are wanted quickly, but are circumscribed in their capabilities of remaining submerged in that spot for long, or of moving fast submerged for more than one attack without rising to recharge their batteries. In submarine design as well as in that of surface ships, you can't have everything; each type is a compromise.

At the other end of the scale we built the R boat. These were also "specialists," but of opposite qualities. Of 500 tons (submerged) they have a surface speed of about eight knots, but a submerged speed of 14½—a speed which will probably be slightly increased by alterations. These boats only joined up in the summer of 1918, and the enemy surrendered before they had really shown what they could do. A boat of this type (they are perfectly stream-lined, and, inside, they are all battery and torpedo tubes) can jog out to her assigned area at her leisure— it is no use sending her to cut off or meet a definitely reported enemy, as she wouldn't get there in time—and once in that area she can use her diving batteries for days without having to recharge them, should she be kept down by enemy hunters, and her high submerged speed and radius make her very dangerous to any target (U-boat or otherwise) which passes within periscope range of her.

There remains the submarine monitor, which will be described in due course. I will interpolate here an account of a typical trial of a new boat, using an E boat of the early 1916 vintage as an illustration.

2

The boat I would use as an illustration was in 1915 very new indeed, She was just a standard E boat, with war-taught improvements and additions, and with a war-taught complement of officers and a half-taught complement of men. For a month the men had been given a queer but useful course of instruction by being taken by their First Lieutenant at "Diving Stations," in a disused shed in the building firm's premises. On the walls and floor names and rough sketches of most of the important valves and wheels of the boat herself had been chalked, and though the men laughed and swore at the make-believe, they had learnt a good deal of their drill and the probable sequence of diving orders, without the work of the builders of the E boat being interfered with.

Except in the dinner hour, or during the infrequent holidays, no drill could be carried out aboard owing to the crowds of men working there. Overtime had been continuously worked, and nothing could be allowed to interfere with the firm's sacred "date"—the day on which the Admiralty had been promised delivery. The day dawned clear and fine, with no wind and every promise of calm spring weather. At six o'clock the submarine's whistle blew shrilly, and a few tardy passengers approaching from the direction of the yard gates broke into a run. As they climbed the iron rungs up to the low grey-painted bridge, the gangway by which they had boarded was lifted clear into the air and swung away to the basin-side by a hissing, clattering, 10-ton crane, and at an order from the boat's captain the securing wires and hemp hawsers splashed into the oily still water.

The telegraph clanged decisively, and to an answering whirr and boil under her stern the boat moved slowly ahead towards the open basin entrance. She increased speed as she neared the narrow passage, and the whirling eddies of a flooding tide outside came in view. As her stem came out into the river she took a sharp sheer upstream, then came quickly round towards the open sea as the twenty degrees of helm that she was carrying took effect on her. Little puffs of white and brown smoke began to show round her stern as the engines were clutched in and started, and in five minutes she was heading down-river at a fair twelve knots, with the low sun glancing from her round hull and lighting the queer mixture of Futurist painting that covered her.

She carried a matter of eleven people on her bridge—a bridge designed to accommodate, perhaps, four or five. Her fighting complement was thirty-one all told, but at this moment she held over fifty. Needless to say, it was the passengers who seemed to take up most room. They comprised overseers, foremen, chargemen, a manager or two, about a dozen caulkers and engineers, and a pilot. In addition she carried an overseer of overseers—a commander from the submarine commodore's staff. He was present as school-master, judge, and as friend to the captain of the boat, and his job was one the captain of the boat was not in the least envious of.

The captain knew that his crew were only partially trained, that he himself was new to E boats, and that the boat might not be all he hoped to find her in the way of reliability and hull-strength, but he felt that at any rate he knew more or less what the personnel, including himself, were like, while the inspecting commander must be, or ought to be, the most nervous man in submarines, with his job of travelling from trial to trial, unbroken by a chance of a trip in a fully-tested boat with a fully-trained crew.

As they swung round the last river-buoy and saw the outer lightship draw clear of the land, a destroyer overtook them, and passed on ahead to lead them to sea. The boat was going thirty miles out to get deep water for her hull-test, and it was not safe for a British boat to be that distance, or even a third of that distance, from the mouth of a British harbour unescorted, unless she was there on her war business. This was not because of the enemy—far from it; it was to save her from the enthusiastic but misguided attentions of the multitudes of "Fritz –hunters" who drew no distinction between submarines of their own or the enemy's flag.

As she neared the light-vessel, the submarine increased speed and some of the "yarning-party" on the bridge departed below down the conning-tower. The programme included a full-speed surface-trial which was to start from the lightship and finish at the diving-ground, and for the next two hours the engineers and engine-overseers were to be the only busy passengers. From the engine-room bulkhead to the bows, the crew and officers moved to and fro—testing, instructing, and, it should be added, grumbling continuously, for the multitude of passengers were a considerable handicap in the way of an efficient and (the great ideal) an unexciting and placid diving-trial.

The inside of the boat was incredibly dirty from a naval point of view. She had not been built at one of these yards where no workman can live without a quid of tobacco in his cheek (in fact by the trials standard of some yards she was clean), but it was obvious that she would take a good month's scrubbing and polishing before she was, in her officers' estimation, even sanitary.

At ten o'clock an order came from on deck, and a couple of sailors ascended the conning-tower carrying a few rounds of 12-pounder ammunition. The trials she was to do were to be complete and to everybody's satisfaction, and the building firm, being a firm which would sooner see their work over- than under-tested, had suggested a few rounds from the bow-gun before the dive, with the idea that if the gun-mounting was going to cause leaks through to the hull as a result of recoil, it should be given the chance to do it now instead of later when the boat was in enemy waters.

A biscuit-tin was dropped, the boat circled round, and at a range of a hundred yards the gunlayer proceeded to miss the box completely. However, the shooting did not matter—the gun had recoiled a few times and that was all that was required. The fact of the gunlayer finding later that he had shipped the sights of the H.A. gun on to his bow-gun before practice, was a merely trifling incident among the errors that one might expect to occur on trials.

At eleven o'clock the destroyer, which had been jogging along a few cables ahead, circled round and slowed up. The submarine captain rang "Slow" on his telegraph, smiled encouragingly at the civilians who still remained on the bridge, and made a pointing gesture with his thumb at the open conning-tower lid. The civilians, with a nervous straightening of bowler hats and several lingering looks at the sunlit sea and sky, clambered slowly below, and the captain remained watching the whirling arms of the semaphore on the destroyer's bridge. He dictated a reply to his signalman, then rang down "Stop," and, leaving the lid open, descended to see what order his first lieutenant was producing out of the crowded chaos below.

From the foot of the conning-tower ladder he could see nothing but a mass of humanity, mostly civilian, through which his uniformed crew moved apologetically and bent double. He moved forward into the crowd and assisted his officers in their efforts to station the passengers in positions where they would be as much out of the way as possible, and would at the same time be comfortable enough to lose their desire to move about. At the end of five minutes comparative peace reigned, and the crew were standing at their stations looking at their officers for orders across a new deck of caps and tilted bowler hats.

The captain took a sweeping glance fore and aft, then ascended the conning-tower. He ordered the signalman below, looked across at the destroyer through his glasses, and then descended, closing and locking the lid above his head. As he re-entered the boat, he caught the eye of the first lieutenant. "Flood one, two, five, six, seven, and eight," he ordered. "Slow ahead both—keep her level."

The vent valves indicated their opening with a snort and a roar of air, and the rush and gurgle of flooding tanks cut off the chatter of the passengers, as the clang of a closing breech-block brings silence to a gun's crew. A few seconds later the Captain spoke again. "Flood three and four—take her down." Each order was repeated by the first lieutenant—an officer whose eyes seemed to note the doings of every man in the boat at once.

As the captain moved to the diving-gauge by the periscope to watch for the first slow movement of the long black needle, the first lieutenant's hand shot out and gripped the neck of a seaman by the starboard pump, and he spoke in a voice of concentrated, hissing rage. "That's the main line, you fool! Close it, quick, and don't you dare touch it till I tell you!"

The gauge-needle quivered and began to rise. At eight feet the captain stepped back, and, taking the periscope training-handles, began to look into the rubber-padded eye-piece, "Check at twenty feet," he said. "Take the angle off now, coxswain."

"Twenty feet, sir, horizontal."

The coxswain sat on a low heavy music-stool facing another white-faced diving-gauge, his big brass hydroplane wheel moving a turn or two each way under his hand. "Pump on Z internal—don't start till I tell you."

The captain was watching the hydroplane helm indicators beside him, which showed, by the amount of "rise" helm they were carrying, that the boat had a touch of negative buoyancy.

"All ready the pump, sir!"

"Start the pump—keep her up, coxswain."

"Coming up, sir—horizontal, sir.'"

"Stop the pump—close main line—close Z internal."

On an even keel the E boat ploughed along—her periscope top four feet above the surface, and the periscope-wake bubbling and foaming on the perfectly smooth sea. The watcher in the following destroyer saw the wake die down till it was a barely visible ripple, as—her trim correct—the captain eased the boat's speed down to less than two knots. Then the shining periscope began to disappear, slowly reducing in height as the planes took the boat down for her deep hull test.

Inside her hull there was silence except for an occasional whisper from one seated civilian to his neighbour. The gauge-needles crept slowly round, and as the depth increased the little spot of daylight thrown by the periscope eye-piece on to the pump-starter abreast of it changed from yellow to green of ever-darkening shades till the last link with the sun above them died away.

At ninety feet the captain spoke again, and the hydroplane-wheels spun as her down-ward way was checked. "Keep her at that," he said. "Mr Ramage, will you send your men round now? We'll mark leaks before we go further."

The foreman addressed rose from his seat and called to his half-dozen caulkers sitting at hand. The boat dived easily on while the men passed fore and aft painting red dabs on rivets and seams overhead where trickles of water spoke of red-lead or packing which was not yet "set" or in condition to face the pressures of active service. Their tour over, the party settled back to their stations, and at a nod and gesture from the captain the hydroplane men tilted the bow slightly down again for further descent. At a hundred and twenty feet the order came for the motors to stop, and with failing headway the boat sank gently down.

One or two men (naval as well as civilian) reached out a hand to grasp for support as they stood, for the moment before touching bottom is always one of slight uncertainty; for, however reliable the chart, it is yet possible to bounce roughly on these occasions on such unexpected obstacles as isolated rocks or even wrecks. But there was no need for bracing against the unexpected today. The boat touched and slid on to a standstill so gently and imperceptibly that her Captain watched the gauge for at least thirty seconds after she had landed, with the suspicion that she might be only "statically trimmed "and that she had a fathom or two farther yet to fall. Then he spoke—"Flood A-hydroplanes amid-ships."

There came a bubbling roar from the vent of A, well forward, and then the clang of a heavy "water-hammer" in the pipe as the tank filled. The boat lay now as he intended her to do, bedded with negative buoyancy and with her bows well down, so that her screws and rudder were clear of the oozy mud in which she lay. "Carry on—all hands—and look for leaks."

The caulkers did not linger over the task. They did not (and small blame to them, for they were not case-hardened to the situation) relish the idea of staying longer than was necessary at a hundred and thirty-six feet by gauge and with a pressure of sixty pounds to the square inch trying to force the round steel hull inwards on itself. In a quarter of an hour they reported "All leaks located and marked."

But their ordeal was not yet over. The gloomy-eyed first lieutenant (a pessimist, as all first lieutenants should be) had found a new leak right aft, and the captain was called into consultation over it. For ten minutes more the two officers conversed and searched, then came leisurely forward again.

"That's all right, I think," said the captain cheerfully. "Anybody want to look round anymore? I can stay down here while they do—there's no hurry, you know."

There was an enthusiastic chorus from a group of overseers and officials—"Not at all, not at all, we're quite satisfied—quite . . ."

The commander, who throughout the dive had sat unmoving by the periscope, notebook in hand and his eyes half closed, allowed himself a faint smile and a lazy yawn.

"Blow on A—fifty pounds—Blow one and two externals."

The air hissed and whined along the pipes, and the eardrums of those aboard tingled to the rising pressure from overloaded relief valves. For five minutes the hissing and roaring continued, then at a shouted order the noise stopped. The first lieutenant looked back from the motionless gauge to the captain. "Shall we put more on A, sir? Fifty pounds won't have moved any out at this depth . . ."

"No—don't put any more on, I've got One and Two pretty near out and the fifty will blow A as she rises. Then I'm going to fill One and Two again and catch the trim before we break surface. She's stuck in the mud, that's all, and we'll have to pull her out. Stand by the motors, aft there!"

The passengers were fidgeting slightly, and the commander, noting the fidgeting, looked up and spoke, laughing, to the youthful captain—*apropos* of absolutely nothing at all. The captain laughed back (for publication and as a guarantee of good faith) and turned to the motor-room voice-pipe: "Slow ahead Port—half ahead Starboard"—a pause filled by a dry humming from right aft where the big motors purred.

"Stop both—slow ahead Starboard—half astern Port"—another droning pause, and then—"Stop Starboard—half astern Starboard."

The boat quivered, then with a lurch she pulled free and her bows rose sharply. "Stop both—half ahead both—flood One and Two—flood A—Dammit—hard-a-dive, coxswain."

The angle increased fast, faster than the forward tanks could fill, and the boat rushed upwards with chests, men, and other loose impediments sliding and slipping aft. At eighty feet she began to level slightly, but the angle could not be taken off her in time,—the destroyer men had a vision of a grey conning-tower foaming ahead for a few seconds, surmounted by fifteen feet of silver periscope, before, to the drive of her powerful screws, the boat dipped again till only the tops of the hooded lenses showed as she settled at her diving depth.

"Rotten" observed the captain gloomily to the first lieutenant. "I mustn't break surface like that when we get to the Bight, or we all go West one-time,—I think that'll do for the dive, though. She'll be tight as a drum when the firm's had another day or two at her. We'll do the helm and speed trials now and then go in. Hands by the blows! Surface!"

3

The Submarine Flotillas began to move to their war bases on the 29th July. By the 4th August they were ready to begin their work. The 8th Flotilla ("D" and "E" boats) were at Harwich, a port which throughout the War has remained the chief Heligoland Bight Patrol base. The "C" boats were spread all up the East Coast, with a Channel guard at Dover and a large number of them at Leith.

The Heligoland Patrol started on the 5th. The boats of the 8th Flotilla not patrolling in the Bight guarded, till the 13th August, a line drawn across the northern entrance of the Channel (between the Belgian and English shoals) till the Expeditionary Force was safely over. During the passage of this force it was fully expected that the enemy would show naval activity and make an attempt to hinder or prevent the passage of troops. Precautionary measures were therefore taken. That the enemy made no attempt to interfere or to dispute the command of the Channel was a surprise to our War Staff, who based their calculations on what an enterprising Naval Power would do in similar circumstances. A possible reason for the enemy's sluggishness at this time is that he does not appear to have at all expected to be at war with England.

From Commodore (S),
To Chief of War Staff, Admiralty.
7th August 1914 (Midnight).
Propose to postpone oversea operations from Yarmouth, and to concentrate all submarines in area arranged until after transit of Expeditionary Force. How many days will passage occupy?

On the 14th the patrol in the Bight continued.
The following despatch is a typical report of an E boat's trip into the Bight during these early days of war:—

H.M. Submarine "E 6,"
15th August 1914.
Sir,—I have the honour to submit a report of the proceedings of Submarine "E 6" on August 6th and 7th, when working in the Heligoland Bight.

August 6th—
1 a.m. Slipped by *Amethyst*, 30— N.N.E. from Terschelling Light vessel, proceeded N. 69 E., twelve knots, making for allotted area, and avoiding T.B.D. patrol.

3 a.m. Dived to check trim; day breaking on rising; sighted two steam trawlers four to five miles to southward; dived away from them; three miles.

4.25 a.m. Proceeded E. x S., twelve knots.

6.30 a.m. Altered course S.E.

7.25 a.m. Sighted German cruiser, *Stettin* class, hull down, E.N.E., beam on, steering N. (approx.). Dived E. by N. one mile to avoid being seen; cruiser too far off to attack.

8.5 a.m. Rose. Sighted trail of smoke and yellow funnel, E.N.E.
Dived to attack, course N. 30 W., full speed.

8.55 a.m. Abandoned chase, enemy steaming very fast west (approx.).
Dived to avoid steam trawler, which had passed over boat during attack.

9.45 a.m. Rose. Proceeded to westward charging batteries.

11.30 a.m. Stopped. Charged on surface.

1.15 p.m. Proceeded S. 72 E., twelve knots.

2.45 p.m. Dived to avoid steam trawler, remaining on course S. 72 E.

3.40 p.m. Rose.

3.50 p.m. Sighted German large T.B.D., or flotilla cruiser, ten miles to northward, steaming very fast E. Too far off to attack.

4.15 p.m. Proceeded S. 51 E., twelve knots.

5.45 p.m. Position W. ¾ N. 23—from Heligoland. Nothing in sight except numerous trawlers, chiefly sailing. Turned to N. 60 W., nine knots. Sea rough.

8.10 p.m. Increased to 10½ knots. Many trawlers in sight at nightfall.

9.30 p.m. Stopped. Dived 50 feet on "grouper down" till—

August 7th—
2 a.m. Rose. Very dark; dived 50 feet.

3.15 a.m. Rose.

3.30 a.m. Proceeded under one engine, eight knots, working round a large fleet of sailing trawlers making to southward; making for route of warships seen yesterday.

6 a.m. Altered course twelve knots.

7.45 a.m. Altered course S.E.

8.15 a.m. Sighted German submarine on surface, S.E. four to five miles distant, beam to beam. Dived to attack. At first thought she was stopped and had then dived, not sighting her through periscope till 8.45.

8.45. a.m. Sighted her steaming west, four or five miles off. Followed, diving.

9.30 a.m. Rose. Submarine not in sight. Followed, diving, for ¾ hour, in hopes of finding her stopped.

10.30 a.m. Proceeded S. 56 E., twelve knots.

12 noon. Stopped to let steam trawler pass across horizon, ahead.

Note.—Since about 7 a.m. I had given up the idea of trying to keep out of sight of trawlers, merely avoiding going within a mile of them.

12.10 p.m. Proceeded.

12.54 p.m. Altered course south, observed position being further north than intended. The steam trawler sighted at noon seemed suspicious of E 6, altering course so as to keep me in sight without getting close.

3.30 p.m. Turned and steered for trawler, signalling her to show colours (German), and to stop. Trawler fitted with W/T. Crossed her bows and shaped course N. 87 W., fourteen knots. Position then N. 43 W. 37—from Heligoland. Trawler proceeded, apparently shaping course for *Emden*. Steered to avoid our T.B.D. patrol.

August 8th—
6.30 a.m. Made Swarte Bank Light-vessel. Proceeded to Lowestoft to report.

Note.—The Heligoland Bight contained a very large

number of trawlers, chiefly sailing, including a few which were apparently Dutch; they became more numerous closer in to Heligoland. I did not notice W/T in any except the one I spoke.

I have the honour to be, sir, your obedient servant,

(Sd.) G. P. Talbot,
Lieutenant-Commander.

The Commodore (S),
H.M.S. *Maidstone*.

That is the sort of way the submarine officers describe their experiences. The method is curt and unsatisfying somehow. I will try and give an idea of a submarine captain describing a trip during, say, the winter of 1915-1916, to an army brother:—

"Yes, we got in yesterday. No—we had no luck. It's getting dull inside there now; it's not so much fun if there are no big ships about and only small craft chasing you. Well, you see, we left about 4 p.m. on Monday and had a poor sort of trip across—blowing from the north-east, so that we were head to sea, and even at eight knots we took nearly every wave over the bridge. They're a fine sight though, the E boats, when they're butting into it like that; they get out of step so, and you can feel just about when they are going to take a good one; you see more and more of her bow going dry as she goes wrong, and then she puts a great length of herself over a hollow, and that's the time to duck your head and hold tight to a rail, because she comes down wallop just in time for the next one to roll right over you.

"It was fairly clear, but devilish cold, and there were snow-squalls about one to the half-hour. We gave Terschelling (the corner, you know, round Holland into the Bight) a seventeen-mile berth, as the tide sets in pretty strong there, and turned in for our billet. My orders were to work between Heligoland and the mouth of the Elbe. There are two ways of getting in, you see—close along the shore in seven-ten fathom water, and over and under the minefields farther out. We took the deep channel, as we don't do the other at night if we can help it—over and under?

"Oh! you see, there's a minefield set for submarines in one place—fairly deep laid, and farther on another set for surface ships, so we go over one and dive under the other—anyhow, they're both only reported fields, and their position isn't accurately known, and also one doesn't quite know one's position if one doesn't get sights or see Terschelling Light, so it's a matter of luck, really. Well, we didn't get any excitements going in, except that my R.N.R. officer pressed the button with his shoulder when he was coming up to relieve me, and he and I only got down just in time to shut the lid. You see, we run with mighty little buoyancy on patrol when we are on the surface, and if you press the button you go down in a few seconds at twelve knots or so.

"The button? why, that's what dives the boat; if you press that (it's just under the conning-tower lid) it rings the Klaxon horns fore and aft the boat, and then it's up to you to come down quick because the crew know it means business, and they don't waste any time. They open all vents and put her nose down, and in a few seconds there's just a 'plop' on the surface and you're looking at a gauge-needle going round down below. But if you come on watch with too many lammies and clothes on, you may give the alarm by mistake like my feller did.

"Well, we got better weather after we rounded Terschelling, and after Borkum Riff it was nearly calm. We got to the billet and dived at 4 a.m.—thirty-six hours out from Harwich. The soundings were right when we touched bottom—about 95 feet—so that checked our latitude a bit. Then we all went to bed. It was pretty cold and jolly wet too, as she leaks a bit overhead besides the usual sweating. What's sweating? Why, when the hull's cold it sweats, you know—water runs down the inside—condensation really, I suppose.

"Well, then we all turned in, as I say, and I put a lot of blankets over me to dry my wet clothes. . . . I was too tired to change, and as a result I was all aches in the morning (that is, at daylight about three hours later). I reckoned it would be getting grey about seven, so we rose then, and after a few minutes at fifty feet, just to listen for propellers, we broke surface. It was all clear and still fairly dark, so we charged batteries for twenty minutes and ventilated.

"Then we went under and started diving patrol. I took first periscope watch, as I wanted to fix position by steering north-west for Heligoland. At eight o'clock the patrol trawlers came by. You see, they have eighteen trawlers out between Schillig Road and the Island. They work in pairs, each pair doing a sort of sword-dance, and making Saint Andrew's Crosses along the line. They come out in the morning, and we just sheer out of their way to let them by. Then at sunset they all begin edging towards home (that's Wilhelmshaven), until the senior one hoists a signal, and they speed up and hustle into bed.

"No, we don't worry them—we haven't enough torpedoes to chuck them away on trawlers; and anyhow, you may miss a chance at something big if you get seen on your patrol. Those small craft don't see you unless you worry them. One dives around all day with several of them in sight, but so long as one doesn't show the periscope much, and doesn't get too close, they don't see. If we once started strafing them, they'd keep a better lookout, but nobody keeps a good look-out unless he's scared—so we don't scare them.

"Well, that's about all we saw that trip. A destroyer passed—out of range—on the third day, going about twenty-five knots, and we had some trouble on the fourth. No, not dangerous, just aggravating. You see, we got seen by some idiot, and they sent out the usual four torpedo-boats in line abreast against us. They're just small high-bowed old boats, and aren't worth a tor-pedo. They came fussing along and saw my periscope at fairly long range, as it was flat calm. I went down to ninety feet, and they let off squibs over us—just little depth charges that didn't even break a light globe.

"Still, they kept me under till dark, and when we came up then I knew I was going to have trouble and worry getting my charge in, as they'd have all sorts of packets barging round my patrol at night looking for me; so we thought it over, and decided the best place to sit and charge would be on the shoals off the Schillig Road boom defences, because they'd never look for us there. Well, they didn't; we sat there and had an absolutely undisturbed charge for the first time that trip. We saw a lot of small craft go by, all heading out to sea to put in a hate against us; and the joke was that we were only in six fathoms there, and couldn't have got the whole boat wet if we had been strafed into diving there. And what's better, I was told today that some of their destroyers looking for us that night had a scrap among themselves—he's such a jumpy feller the Hun: they seemed to have damaged one packet pretty thoroughly, according to the Intelligence people.

"Why do we have to sit up at night? But we don't. We only have to stay up long enough to charge the batteries for next day, and then we pack up and go to the bottom till morning. That's why winter's the best time to patrol—for comfort, anyway. In December you can only see decently through a periscope for about nine hours—then you come up and charge and get to the bottom for dinner. In July it's more like work: you dive twenty-one hours, come up and charge, and dive again about 2.30 a.m. There's no time for a rest on the bottom, but if you're inside the Bight it's quite exciting getting your charge in. You get put down in the middle of the performance by black shapes coming right on top of you.

"They're usually trawlers on patrol; but sometimes you see a big bow wave, and that means a destroyer, and you crash-dive in a few seconds. You see, a boat charging like that is like a crab with its shell off; you never feel safe in a boat until you are submerged. On a clear night you can deal with destroyers or any other craft, but these pitch-black nights, or nights when it is foggy or snowing, are the deuce. I never feel happy on those nights till we get to the bottom. It gives me cold feet all the time when I'm on the surface inside there. This trip we got put down at least once during each charge, except the night I went into their front garden to hide.

"One night, however, I thought we'd never get charged up; we kept getting put under, so that it was a case of twenty minutes' charge and ten minutes' dip for half the night. What's 'putting down' like? Well, you see, when you decide it's dark enough to come up, and you've seen the trawlers go home, you pass the word to 'Stand by for surface' and to get the engines ready. All the hands wake up and get busy (they read and sleep most of the day), and then when they report 'Ready' you blow about five to ten tons out of the tanks, and you come up. There's a routine for the business, you see, and they don't want telling much. I open the lid as soon as it's clear of the surface, and a hand follows me up on to the roof.

"I have a look round, and if it's all clear I sing out below to start the charge. They get on with it then, and the engines start bumping the batteries up full bore, and at the same time we move slow ahead. I only keep just the conning-tower out, and no more buoyancy, so we have men on the hydroplane wheels to keep her from doing a dive accidentally, and as we're moving ahead a little 'up helm' keeps her fairly dry. The hand on deck does 'look-out' astern and I look out ahead; meanwhile the people below carry on smoking (that's the chance they've been waiting for all day).

"If the lookout sees anything at all he gives a yell and points at it, and then jumps down inside the conning-tower. If I don't like it when I turn round and see it, I press the button and follow him down. If I see something first I hit the lookout, and he jumps down and I follow. They're all on the top line below, so as soon as I press the button and the horns sound (they make a din all over the boat) they open the vents and put her bow down with the planes, and then by the time I've closed the lid over my head the gauge is showing fifteen feet, and she's going down at a big slant.

"If I'm slack on the lid. I get wet. If I'm too slack and the first lieutenant thinks I'm not going to get the top lid shut before she's under, he slams the lower doors and either leaves me isolated in the tower or else swimming around on the surface till he comes up later to look for me. (No—I've never got left like that yet, but some people have been pretty near it. It's not safe for the first lieutenant to hang on too long for you—he might fill the boat.)

"It's quite simple. With a well-trained crew anything's safe, and you can cut it as fine as you like. When you've heard the propellers from overhead[1] you just keep along at sixty feet for ten minutes or so, and then you come up and get on with the work again. Oh! I'm bored with all this talking. You ought to be able to run a trip inside by yourself by now. But there's one thing always makes me mad, that's the Heligoland leave-boat. She leaves the island on Friday afternoons and she comes back on Monday morning.

"She's a big flat-bottomed coal barge—too shallow draught to torpedo—and crammed with men. You can't use a gun, because she's towed by a small tug with a big gun forward and a little one aft; and besides, we're not allowed to give away the fact that we're there by having a joke with small craft. But it's devilish aggravating, all the same, to see the bloated Hun going off for the weekend while we dive up and down for a week waiting for something to turn up. We get our leave all right though. We get three days to the half crew each trip, so that each of us gets leave every other trip.

"The business is too exciting for me to take leave seriously. I just go to all the revues and amusements I can if I go up to town, and if it's winter-time like now, I get in three days' shooting here. The local people are jolly nice to us, and even if they haven't got a regular shoot going, one can get out to the marshes and shoot duck. After the leave we come back and do a couple of days' exercise-diving and torpedo practice, and then we go out again for another trip.

"It's awfully interesting, because we work in the Huns' front-yard in a way, and it seems so cheeky somehow. Makes us want a drink? Well, I guess not. If you've got cold feet you don't want

---

1 The date the speaker deals with is before the general use of the hydrophones in submarines.—Klaxon.

a drink, because you daren't have it. That's why we don't carry any in the boats. You see, the Owner here looks on us as so many race-horses he's got in training, and if one of us shows symptoms of breathing a bit short, he gets classed as a roarer, and leaves the job altogether to repent in a big ship; there's lots more waiting to take our place, and the Owner's got no what you'd call 'mother-liness,' if he thinks you're not all out for business. Hearing propellers? Oh yes, you can hear them quite clearly from any quiet part of the boat; the fore torpedo compartment is a good place for listening, and so is the space abaft the main motors.

"You can hear what speed he's going, and when you're used to them you can make out what kind of craft he is—trawler or destroyer. The best time, though, is when you've finished a day's patrol and charging and all, and gone on down to the bottom. I allow the whole crew one cigarette apiece, and they have a concert. They gather round the periscope and sing for an hour before turning in, and the orchestra plays—(that's a concertina and a couple of mandolins),—we've got quite a lot of talent in the boats. Smoking like that overnight doesn't matter. If you keep the circulating fans running the smoke all goes away while you're asleep.

"I don't know where it goes to, 'cos it can't get out; but it goes somewhere. I allow the officers a couple of cigarettes apiece during the daytime, and I smoke whenever I feel scared—that gives me about nine cigarettes a day. Of course you can't smoke at the end of a long summer's day; after about fourteen hours' diving you can't get a cigarette to burn, and a match goes out as soon as it's struck. But you can smoke a bit in the forenoon without spoiling the air in the boat—and besides, on occasions like when somebody is chasing you and dropping those little depth bombs they use, and you've gone to ninety feet or so to keep clear of them, it's a sort of guarantee of good faith if the skipper walks away from the periscope and lights a fag.

"It looks contemptuous somehow, and the sailors approve. You see, they never know the facts of what's going on. Only the skipper knows the situation, and so they watch you all the time.

They spend a trip sitting or lying by their stations, and obeying orders and trusting to their boss not to kill them unnecessarily if he can help it. I tell you, the submarine sailor, once he's past his probation time and been tested on patrol, is a hand worth writing home about! Now, if you'll stop listening a minute and struggle out of that chair, I'll take you round the boat. She's pretty filthy still, but we'll get her clean again by tomorrow."

CHAPTER 2

Anti-Submarine Work

1

Before speaking of anti-submarine work, a very short description of the German submarine and its variations in type is advisable.

A U-boat is not unlike our ordinary patrol-type submarine. She varies in size and capabilities, but is generally a 16-knot (surface speed) boat, with two guns—a 4·1-inch and a 22-pdr., two bow and two stern torpedo-tubes, and about 800 tons surface displacement.

A U-B boat is a small patrol boat of about 500 tons surface displacement; one 4·1-inch or 22-pdr. gun, one stern and four bow torpedo-tubes, 13 knots surface speed. There is also a "Flanders," type U-B class, of 250 tons and 8½ knots speed. The latter class worked from Ostend and Zeebrugge.

A U-C boat is about 400 tons; one 22-pdr. gun, twelve knots speed, one stern and two bow torpedo-tubes. The Flanders type U-C's are of 180 tons and 7½ knots speed. All U-C's are primarily fitted for mine-laying.

The U cruisers are from 2000 to 3000 tons displacement, carry two 5·9-inch guns, have a speed of sixteen knots, and in some cases are fitted as mine-layers in addition to their torpedo equipment.

The number of slight divergences from the main types is considerable. Boats were built in standardised groups, and, during the second half of the war, in great quantities. On November

11th, 1918, the position was, roughly, as follows: 200 submarines in German hands, commissioned or completing—135 (roughly) on the building slips. About 200 had been destroyed up to that date.

In 1918 the average number of German submarines at sea—in the Adriatic, Irish Sea, Channel, and North Sea—was (in the spring) 20, in October, 24. The number available for service—excluding Mediterranean boats, school boats, and boats out of date—was about 72; so that, roughly, one-third were kept at sea, and the remainder resting or repairing.

The medium-size German submarines are quite good-looking boats, but the German mind showed itself clearly in the U cruisers. It has been an axiom at sea since the days of the Vikings, that a thing that looks ugly isn't good seamanship. British submarines are better streamlined than German boats, and have generally a more "varminty" and clean-run look.

The sight of a U cruiser in dry dock recalls to one's mind a pair of pictures once published in *La Vie Parisienne*—a Paris weekly which has done as much to win the war as any other periodical. The first picture showed a "seventy-five" gun, and standing beside it a girl built on clearly thoroughbred lines, balancing a cartridge on her hand. The second was of a squat 11-inch howitzer, accompanied by *La Vie's* interpretation of a homely German *frau* clutching the great shell to her portly figure. The two pictures illustrate rather well the ideas of our own K-boat designers as compared with the mental state of the authors of the German submarine cruisers.

2

It used to be a catchword of naval correspondents that "submarine cannot fight submarine." Well, it is true, and it isn't. What can be done is that one submarine submerged can torpedo another submarine on the surface: in which case submarine No. 2 is not really a submarine at the moment. Two submarines may meet and have a gun-action, with possible damage to one or both of them, and much entertainment to their crews; but in such a case neither boat would be acting as a submarine.

Throughout the war our boats have been on the look-out for, and ready to engage, any enemy submarines met with. We have had boats, in varying numbers, since the middle of 1915 engaged definitely in submarine-hunting—that is, those boats that could be spared from the all-important task of watching the Bight and its approaches. The anti-submarine boats we sent out simply proceeded to areas where, by inference or by "information received," U-boats might be expected to be working. The ordinary patrol boats on passage to and from their stations, or while watching at their stations for the coming of big ships, often met with U-boats, and naturally took the chances the gods gave them with gun, torpedo, stem, or whatever means seemed best at the moment.

Of course, the torpedo was the usual weapon used. A hit on a big ship, once the destroyer screen has been avoided, is comparatively easy; a hit on a U-boat is mighty difficult. The attacker is looking at his target with his eye (the top prism of the periscope) only a few inches above water-level. His view of the enemy, therefore, is confined to a square-looking conning-tower, with heavy "jumping wires" (sweep deflectors) running down from it to a low grey line of hull.

It is therefore difficult to exactly estimate the enemy's speed or course, and the short time at the attacker's disposal for deciding on his deflection and turning to bring his tubes to bear does not allow of an accurate calculation based on bearings of the passing target. In fact, it is usually a case of "make up your mind and shoot quick."

In addition to the handicap of the target being small, there is the knowledge that one must be far more careful to show only a little of the periscope during the attack, as submarines are far more on the *qui vive* for periscopes than big ships are. For one thing, they know what a periscope looks like; and for another, they have more knowledge of what a torpedo can do against craft of small buoyancy.

The moral effect of the use of submarine against submarine was probably greater than the direct effect. It discouraged U-boats from coming to the surface to use their guns against merchant ships, and restricted them to their torpedo armament, which was of course limited. A U-boat on the surface had the same sensations as a man would have who fell overboard crossing the Indian Ocean, where the sharks are always keeping station astern of a ship: a feeling of impatience, and anxiety to get back to where he came from.

As an instance, I will mention the case of U 81, who, while engaged in the congenial work of pumping shells into an English merchant ship, received two torpedoes amidships from "E 54," who had been following operations through her periscope since U 81 first rose to the surface. "E 54" picked up seven survivors, one of whom was the captain. The latter officer was somewhat damaged by the explosions, and was in danger of drowning until "E 54's" first lieutenant dived for him and brought him aboard. Another survivor was the warrant officer, who, on being taken below, sent a message by "E 54's" coxswain to Commander Raikes, to the effect that it was advisable to keep a good lookout and to submerge again soon, as there was another U-boat diving near at hand. Commander Raikes would no doubt have acted on the second part of this excellent advice had it not been necessary for him to assist the damaged steamer into harbour.

If one once begins to quote cases, it is difficult to keep from irrelevance, but I must note here that at the moment of the sinking of U 81, the crew of the steamer had very wisely abandoned ship, and the change from a U boat in full view to a *ditto* E boat took place so suddenly that there was a natural misunderstanding when "E 54" stood over to tow the boats back to their ship. The steamer's crew were living too fast in twenty minutes for the situation to be quite clear, and in view of their knowledge of the way in which certain U-boats had dealt with survivors, the fact that "E 54" had to actually chase the lifeboats is comprehensible.

The following is from reports of captured U-boat's men:—

Several prisoners give clear evidence of the fear inspired

by the possible presence of Allied submarines submerged when they themselves were on the surface. Besides the probable results of this method of attack, the apprehension of it constitutes a seriously demoralising influence.

From an officer:—

We knew that for every boat we had working in an area, you had two looking for us.

The latter statement shows an error in the officer's calculations. The odds were very much the other way; but his error shows that moral effect goes for a good deal in war.

In actions between submarines, guns have also been used, as have rifles, pistols, and—at short range in the dark—verbal abuse; but no definite sinkings on either side can be traced to these causes. In our boats it was the rule to attack submerged, if possible—in the U-boats it was rare to find an inclination to pursue a gun-action to its logical end. A submarine, when nearly hit, can refuse action at any time by diving. This, of course, forces the opponent left on the surface to dive also, as it would be unhealthy then to remain on the surface in that locality.

Our submarines were always more lightly gunned than the U-boats. Few of them carried more than one small gun—and that one usually an anti-aircraft weapon. This was for two reasons. Firstly, our boats are meant for warship-destroying as opposed to commerce-destroying. The attacking of warships implies speed under water (one should have, roughly, at least half the speed of the class of ship one is after). Big guns are bad for steam-line, and therefore militate against high submerged speed. Secondly, we were supplying guns to Allies, our own Army, and to all our merchant ships and 'mystery ships," and the submarines had to take their turn at the supply with the rest.

The British officer always had an inclination to use the ram if he got a chance. A submarine can ram almost anything, and still, as the U.S. Navy puts it, "Get away with it." Our boats have a ten-inch razor-edged cast-steel stem fitted to them for net-cutting and other purposes. They can also, by their system of compartments, stand damage forward to the extent of a crushed bow, as far back as the bow hydroplanes, with no great risk to themselves. Add to these things the delightful idea of being able to thoroughly damage your ship and to be praised instead of court-martialled for the action, and it is obvious that a number of attempts along this line have been made. There is no record of one having been successful to the extent of sinking an enemy, but in some cases U-boats were damaged in this way.

A curious case of accidental ramming was that in which "E 50" (Lieutenant-Commander Michell), when diving near the N. Hinder Light-vessel, sighted a periscope close aboard on the bow. A moment later the two boats collided heavily at 25 feet by gauge. "E 50's" captain, deciding that the other boat was underneath him, put his hydroplanes "hard-to-dive," and flooded tanks with the idea of carrying the enemy to the bottom (at that point 180 feet away) and crushing him. The U-boat, however, broke away, and after showing her stern and conning-tower a moment on the surface, sank again.

It was later discovered that the enemy got home damaged. "E 50" came out of the affair with the loss of her port-bow hydroplane and a few dents. On such an occasion, there is no time to inspect your own boat for damage before making up your mind if you should or should not instantly rise to the surface. It is a natural action to bring your own boat up as soon as possible, in case the chance of ever getting her up at all goes by. The Captain of "E 50" acted on the rule that a dead U-boat is a primary consideration, whatever one's natural inclinations may be; his crew, though not consulted, were in full agreement with him.

Again, I must quote an irrelevant incident. There were two of our submarines in the Heligoland Bight patrol, diving in adjacent areas. They both returned to harbour slightly damaged— one under the impression that, while diving at 55 feet, he had been run over by a surface vessel; the other reporting that, while diving at 25 feet, he had bumped over a submarine. On meeting in harbour they found the times of the mysterious collisions tallied to the minute.

In April 1915, the idea of using a fishing trawler as a decoy originated in the *Vulcan's* flotilla (C-class submarines)—based on Leith. The U-boats had been sinking our fishing-boats at their leisure, and it was clear that if a few U-boats were mysteriously lost on this duty, it would be a discouraging thought for the remainder. It must be remembered that a "missing" boat has a certain moral effect—a boat openly sunk by gun fire, etc., serves only as an example for others to be more careful.

If a certain duty or a certain area becomes unhealthy for U-boats without any explanation, it tends to make the enemy chary of sending boats out on similar work, until the matter is cleared up. Hence the secretiveness of the Admiralty during the war on the losses of enemy submarines. Prisoners taken from U-boats were prevented from explaining to anybody how their boats were sunk. It may have been from humanity, or it may have been from the consideration that U-boat prisoners were usually communicative in a useful way, but orders were strict that as many prisoners as possible were to be saved from the water when U-boats were sunk.

The *Vulcan's* idea was of masterly simplicity. The U-boats found a fishing fleet easy prey; therefore a fishing fleet with a "catch" on it would get results. One trawler of each fleet was to tow, instead of a trawl, a C-class submarine. The submarine would keep well submerged at the end of the hawser, and need not necessarily keep a periscope lookout, in view of the fact that the critical moment for her to slip tow (a tow can be slipped while submerged) would be notified to her by telephone from the trawler's bridge. Submarine "C 24" was the first to show that the theory worked out in practice.

It will be seen, however, that she did the work under a considerable handicap, and had the most aggravating experience a submarine can have—that of doing an attack with "something wrong with the works."

Lieutenant Taylor, in command, reported:—

At 9.30 a.m., June 23rd, I heard a report which I took to be an explosive signal from trawler *Taranaki* to show my periscope, I being at 30 feet. I telephoned her for confirmation and got the answer, 'Submarine 1500 yards on port bow'; and then again, as trawler altered course, 'Submarine 1000 yards astern.'

I gave the order to slip, but the slipping gear jammed in 'C 24.' I then told *Taranaki* to slip her end, which she did. I went ahead, helm hard a-starboard, to attack submarine astern. The boat immediately sank to 38 feet with 5° inclination, bow down. The trim then took some time to adjust, as I had at that time 100 fathoms of 3½-inch wire hawser, 100 fathom 8-inch coir hawser, and 100 fathom telephone cable hanging from the bows. Eventually sighted enemy's conning-tower 1000 yards off.

Closed to 500 yards, manoeuvred for beam shot, and fired 9.55 a.m. Torpedo hit enemy amidships. I then came to the surface and picked up 'U 40's' captain. My propeller then refused to move, and it was found that there were twenty turns of telephone cable round the shaft . . .

Lieutenant-Commander Edwards (in trawler *Taranaki*) was, of course, ignorant of the fact that "C 24" was somewhat hampered by these cables hanging at the bow:—

. . . 9.30 a.m., June 23rd: Enemy submarine rose and fired a shot across my bows from 2000 yards range—shell burst 20 yards ahead—informed 'C 24' by telephone. 9.45: Slipped *Taranaki's* end of tow, as 'C 24's' slip had jammed. Got boat out to simulate abandoning ship and panic. Saw 'C 24's' periscope pass, attacking. 9.55: Observed torpedo run and explode under conning-tower of enemy. An officer and a petty officer the only survivors . .

Lieutenant-Commander Dobson, in command of "C 27," has an abrupt and almost *blasé* report to make of his sinking of "U 23":—

7.55 a.m., July 20th: Lieutenant Cantlie in trawler *Princess Louise* telephoned to me that a hostile submarine was in sight 2000 yards on the port bow—telling me not to slip for a little while. Telephone then broke down [It would—of course].

At 8 a.m. I heard the sound of shots falling on the water and decided to slip, which I did. Turned to starboard to get clear of trawler and came to 18 feet for a look. Closed enemy to 500 yards, and fired port tube at 8.12. As I fired I observed enemy start her engines, and torpedo missed astern. I shifted my deflection and fired the starboard tube. Torpedo hit the submarine just abaft the conning-tower. I blew main ballast tanks and picked up seven survivors (captain, two officers, and four men). The weather being too bad to get in tow again, I returned to harbour.

Lieutenant Cantlie, in the trawler, reports:—

7.55 a.m., July 20: Sighted hostile submarine three points on port bow, distant 2500 yards—informed 'C 27,' and told her not to slip yet. Hostile submarine steering across my bows. 7.56: Enemy opened fire, apparently trying to hit trawler. Telephone to 'C 27' broke down. 8.3 a.m.: Tow slipped. Enemy fired about seven shots altogether. Employed trawler's crew in hoisting out boat, rushing about the deck, and appearing to be in a panic.

8.10 a.m.: Observed 'C 27's' periscope on starboard quarter attacking enemy. 8.12 a.m.: Observed 'C 27' fire a torpedo, which missed astern. Cleared away starboard gun for action. Enemy opened fire again on trawler, and commenced turning to port. I opened fire with my starboard gun, hoisting white ensign at the main. At the same moment second torpedo hit just abaft enemy's conning-tower. Column of water and smoke rose about 80 feet high. As it cleared away 30 feet of bow of submarine at a large angle could be seen. . . .

The success of this scheme of U-boat hunting depended, of course, entirely on the secrecy maintained as to its existence; it was therefore unfortunate that the prisoners from U 23 were allowed to mix with interned German civilians who were about to be repatriated—a mistake which was excusable in the midst of the general confusion caused in the authorities' minds by the change from peace to war. At that date the disposal of prisoners was out of the Admiralty's hands, and on this mistake being discovered, steps were taken that prisoners having secrets to tell should be prevented from telling them to Germany. The trawler scheme of hunting, however, had to be given up for some time.

In 1916 U-boats again became active against the fishing fleets on the Dogger, and C boats were again sent out to work with the trawlers. On August 28, "C 29" (Lieutenant Schofield), while being towed submerged, struck a mine off the Humber and was lost with all hands. The method was continued for a few more trips, but the U-boats being by then too careful, it was abandoned before the end of the year.

There were eighteen German boats in all sunk by torpedoes from our submarines, while others were hit but were able to get home. I will try to imagine a typical case of submarine v. submarine, in order to give an idea of what lies behind the bare despatches of the victors.

3

The E boat was working a "beat" ten miles to the north of the North Dogger Bank Lightship—a dull beat, too, as in 1918 the U-boat captains had long ago given up the idea of passing near lightships in surface trim. The patrol was not there for enemy submarine strafing, however. The E boat was a unit of the watching semicircle that dived eternally, from the Haaks Light off the Dutch coast to Hiorn's Reef off Jutland, watching for a cloud of smoke to the east that would tell of the coming of the High Sea Fleet.

The boat had been on the billet two days, and had five more to wait before she started her run home to Harwich. She had spent the short spring night jogging about on the surface at six knots, charging her batteries, and at 4 a.m. she slowed up and slipped under. It was her thirtieth patrol trip, and she expected it to be as dull as most of the others had been; there was a kind of yawning, done-it-all-before air in the way the crew took her under that morning, that showed, besides good training, a familiarity with intricate mechanism that had developed into something approaching contempt.

The boat settled to her day's dive at twenty feet, her periscope moving slowly along at a speed of about two knots, leaving a very faint rippling line on the smooth North Sea surface. The captain swung the periscope round, wiped the eye-piece with a nominally clean chamois-leather pad, and then leaned back against the diving gauge, finishing the fag-end of a cigarette.

It was still twilight in the world above him, and the bad light, combined with the fact that periscopes are very apt to "fog" for some minutes after diving, when the engines are still hot enough to make the air in the boat steamy, would prevent him seeing anything clearly for twenty minutes. It was a rule of his to keep the early morning periscope watch himself, as he believed that if anything exciting was going to happen it would always occur at dawn. Certainly, as far as U-boats go, his ideas were right, as a boat on passage is humanly liable to hold on to her surface speed and trim as long as there is a hint of darkness left to protect her, and in submarine war it is the one that gets under earliest that lives longest.

The captain took another look through the periscope, and saw the familiar level floor of the sea blending with the pink and grey of the dawn just as he had seen it on so many previous mornings. He looked forward along his boat and saw the sleeping forms of sailors all the way along the battery deck cloths till his eye was attracted by a pair of sea-boots that projected through the gap in the wardroom curtain. Those were his first lieutenant's boots, and his first lieutenant, he knew well, was snoring loudly beyond them. He threw his cigarette end impatiently down the periscope well and began slowly moving the heavy periscope round, shuffling around with it as he swept the clearing horizon.

It seemed a silly thing to be keeping the morning watch, of all watches, when he had two young and lazy officers to work for him. Their eyes were younger than his, and his were more valuable to the country anyway. It seemed absurd that only he and four "diving hands" should be awake, while all the rest snored. Why should he, an experienced and skilled officer, be at work at half-past four on a dull morning? Why, when he was a junior lieutenant . . . he straightened up from the eyepiece. . . .

"Call the First Lieutenant!"

An hour later the situation in the E boat was the same, except for the fact that a gloomy officer in a soiled sweater and a pair of still more soiled grey flannel trousers plodded round the periscope pedestal, while a pair of stockinged feet showing through the curtain showed whither the captain's train of thought had led him. The crew still dozed fore and aft the boat. At regular intervals the hydroplane motors buzzed noisily as a turn of the wheels corrected her depth; from right aft came the monotonous ticking of a main motor that slowly turned the port propeller and urged the boat lazily along.

In the wardroom the captain, supremely oblivious to a monotonous drip of leaking water from a seam directly over his out-thrown left hand, was back in the days before the war, when the Berkeley Hounds had had three forty-five minute bursts in a day, and he had ridden all three on the same horse. In his dreams he seemed to hear the drumming of many horses' hoofs on the sloping pastures, and the clash and tinkle of stirrups touching as the crowded field fought for room at the first fence. Then he woke and lay propped on one elbow, with a leg thrown over the side of his bunk, while his heart missed two complete beats.

He had not heard the order of "action stations," that came from the periscope position, but he knew well the only possible order that could send men rushing past him to man the bow tubes. He pulled his sea-boots on as he sat up, then jumped down and covered the distance aft to the periscope in half a dozen swift strides. The first lieutenant, his face alight with suppressed emotions, stepped clear and spoke: "Fritz—bow-on, I think—big one"—then dashed forward to superintend the men at the bow tubes.

All along the boat a clatter and ring of metal on metal told of preparation for firing. Amid-ships a hiss and splutter of air showed that the beam tubes were flooding, till a spurt of water coincided with a sharp cry of "Tubes full, sir!" The captain spoke into the voice-pipe at his side, and the ticking sound from the main motors rose to a steady hum. He lowered the periscope till the eyepiece was level with the deck, and stood drumming his fingers against the hoisting wires. The matter of seeing the tubes cleared away and of keeping the boat's trim right lay now with his officers.

His head was to be concerned only with the attack and the shot. He alone would be to blame for a miss now, and he had too well-trained a staff for him to need to worry over any diving details during an attack. His brain was working outside the boat in the early sunshine, where a big and confident U-boat was bound out for her station in the Irish Sea. The enemy was heading straight at him, and he himself was crossing her bow from port to starboard, heading north. To get his bow tubes to bear meant a quick rush to the north to get to a fair range, and then a turn to port till his head was south and the enemy ran across his sights.

He was, in view of the glassy state of the sea, keeping his periscope out of sight as long as possible, and intended to keep the instrument lowered till, on his estimate of the U-boat's course and speed (gauged in his first rapid glance) and his submarine sixth sense, he had turned inwards from a point on his target's starboard bow. In sixty-five seconds from the first sighting of the enemy, peace and quiet reigned again in the E boat. Except for the occasional slight hiss and gurgle as a tube-vent was tested, there was no sign to tell that the whole boat was on a tiptoe of expectant emotion.

Three minutes from his first order to increase speed he starboarded his helm and—still with his periscope lowered—began his turn through west to south. His hands fidgeted now on the taut hoisting wires before him, and every nerve in his body cried for a glance at the enemy just to check his mental estimate. His first glance when his turn was half through would show him whether he had judged rightly, or whether he had made a miscalculation which would be heavy on his soul till the end of his days. But his nerves were well in hand and his will strong; the repeater of the gyroscopic compass had ticked slowly round under his gaze until it showed 275°—a trifle north of west.

Then the periscope rose with a sigh and a creak of straining wires. He stooped and pressed his eye to the instrument as it rose, waiting for the very earliest glimpse of the upper world. All along the boat the men leaned from their stations to watch, for they knew exactly what depended on the quick decision based on that first glimpse he had taken. To his eye the green flickering circle lightened, paled, and then changed to a clear pale-blue sky and a sparkling stretch of sea. He had hoisted the periscope trained to south-west by south, and his heart gave a jump in gratitude to the training that had given him brains to judge rightly.

The U-boat—very near and big—with a little foaming line falling away from her bows, was sailing slowly across the periscope, and he winced as he saw on her bridge the little group of figures that seemed to be looking straight at his face. Instantly he lowered the periscope and forced himself—for he felt that he ought to whisper, in fear of his enemy hearing—to shout the order to "stand by bow tubes." A few seconds later he spoke again as the periscope rose—"Midships—steady on one-eight-five—stop starboard."

As the surface view showed again he carefully jerked the great instrument a fraction round as he set it at his "deflection"—the angle of lead ahead of the enemy, based on a guess at her speed, that corresponds to the "swing in front" of a rabbit-shooter. Then he lowered his hands from the training-handles lest he should be tempted to move the instrument again, and with the order to fire trembling on his lips, waited as the grey stem of the U-boat slid evenly into the view, and the conning-tower and the vertical spider-hair line that formed his actual sight drew together.

At the bow tubes three men and an officer crouched, the pulses of certainly one of them working at abnormal pressure. The actual firing of the tubes would come suddenly, electrically controlled by the Captain sixty feet away. Thud! the port bow torpedo left with a faint roar and rattle—Thud! the heavy ball of the starboard firing-gear came down decisively, and another "18-inch short range—high speed setting" went away on its last run. Two men by the tubes jerked up the vents to let the water rush back into the space that the torpedoes had left vacant, and each of the crouching group held his breath in agonising expectation.

It was really only ten seconds (but it must have felt like a hundred) before the great question was answered: and the answer was savagely and brutally clear. A great clanging report shook the E boat, and the hull quivered as if she had lightly touched something forward. A torpedo man leaned across and closed the two spouting tube-vents, then looked aft and, grinning with relief, sang a *pæan* of victory along the glittering tunnel of the E boat—"Wow!" he said. "Good-bye-ee-ee!"

4

The sinking of U-C 65 by "C 15" (Lieutenant E. H. Dolphin) provides an odd case. There is a story behind the official despatch:—

> 2.43 p.m.: Sighted enemy submarine on the surface five points on the port bow. Dived and flooded both tubes.
> 3.12: Sighted submarine in periscope steering estimated course of N. 70 E, bearing 40° on starboard bow.
> 3.15: Fired double shot at 400 yards—one torpedo hit-the other appeared to pass under.
> Submarine sank immediately—noise of explosion slight.
> 3.17: Surface—picked up five survivors of U-C 65.

The position was about 25—south of Beachy Head. "C 15" was on patrol in rather misty weather, and at the time of sighting the enemy both boats were on the surface, U-C 65 steering home up Channel, "C 15" steering N. by E. across her bows. Both boats saw each other at the same time, and the German watched the English boat go under to attack. The obvious reply was to either dive also or to alter course and pass round the "danger-radius" of the torpedoes on the surface.

The German captain had two mental handicaps—over-confidence and (having just finished a long trip) over-anxiety to get home on leave. He decided not to alter course or delay his passage, but explained to his first lieutenant that it was quite easy to dodge a torpedo if a good look-out was kept and the helm moved quickly. The first lieutenant appears to have had philosophic doubts as to the wisdom, of the proceeding, his doubting being justified when, on seeing the firing-splash as "C 15" fired, the captain neatly dodged one torpedo and received the other fairly amidships.

Lieutenant Dolphin had fired two—"spread" slightly for deflection; not having "declared to win" with either, the question of which one hit did not trouble him. U-C 65 probably won a moral victory, but—"C 15" sank her.

The C boats working round the N. Hinder Light-vessel were liable to make sudden "contacts" with the enemy, usually in thick weather or at night. Both sides would be trying to make the lightship to fix their positions, and on occasions two belligerent submarines would make the lightship together.

On March 1st, 1917, "C 19" (Lieutenant A. C. Bennett) was steering east from the Hinder Light, when she sighted (by moonlight) a small submarine right ahead steering straight at her. "C 19" decided that this looked like another British C boat, several of which were in the vicinity. Each boat turned to north and flashed a challenge.

The German then made I.M.I, (the Morse signal to "repeat," common knowledge to all nations). The boats were then beam to beam at 100 yards' range, and the German hailed in his own language. "C 19" had no gun, and was trying to swing round to bring the bow tubes to bear, having no doubt as to what to do in the matter. The enemy continued to make I.M.I., and turned away to get out of the line of fire. This made it a stern-chase with "C 19" close up and gaining; the German then fired a star-shell, and "C 19" replied with rifles and automatic pistols. That was too much for the Hun; he kicked his tail up and dived, with the bullets smacking on his conning-tower as he went, and "C 19's" starboard torpedo—fired as he dived—racing over the top of him.

The U-boat's periscope showed once on the bow, and "C 19" turned to ram and passed over it, without, unfortunately, hitting anything solid. "C 19," on the 5th March, met another Flanders Flotilla boat, this time with a heavy sea running, which prevented torpedoes being fired with any hope of accuracy. The C boat charged at once, using rifles and pistols as she came in. The enemy dived, and "C 19" passed over her, the bump being slightly felt below. It is possible that the German's periscope was damaged, but he saved his skin by getting under in time.

On the 14th May 1917, in thick weather, "C 6" (Lieutenant Brookes) was feeling for the Hinder Light-vessel. She found it at 7.30 a.m. close aboard, and at the same time a German sub-marine found it, and, appearing 300 yards away, dived at once. "C 6" went under also and pursued by the use of hydro-phones. In about half an hour the enemy's motors were heard to slow up and stop, and "C 6," thinking he had gone to the bottom to avoid the chase, came to the surface to get the mast down, as it had been left standing in the hurry of getting under.

The visibility was only 200 yards, and there was nothing in sight. "C 6" dived again, and, as she did so, heard the rattle and hum of propellers as a torpedo missed her over the top. The German had evidently come up for a look instead of taking bottom. The exasperated "C 6" pursued by hydrophone for an-other quarter of an hour, but the sound of the enemy's motors was then lost.

The list of "Contacts" with enemy submarines shows that in seven cases the enemy was sunk less than five miles from a headland or navigational mark. When proceeding between mine-fields, or when bound for dangerous waters, it is natural for submarines to get a good departure or landfall if possible, but all such strategic points are unhealthy to approach. The following two cases illustrate this. In each of them the U-boat captain closed a light in order to get a good navigational departure, and in each case his precaution had fatal results:—

On the 5th April 1917, "C 7" (Lieutenant A. W. Forbes) was waiting at the Schouwen Bank gas-buoy, watching the channel that led to Zeebrugge. She lay on the surface with half-buoyancy, and was undoubtedly, as can be guessed from the despatch, on the "top-line" in the matter of being ready for action. Lieutenant Forbes' first lieutenant was on the sick-list most of the trip, so that he himself was pretty well worn out on his return to harbour by continual watch-keeping and anxiety.

3.32 a.m.: Sighted submarine on port quarter steering about north, distant 400 yards. Turned and at once fired port torpedo at a range of about 250 yards. Torpedo hit forward with loud explosion, sending up a large column of water. Submarine turned to port and sank in a few seconds. The night was very dark and misty, and no survivors or debris could be seen.

In "E 52's" (Lieutenant P. Phillips) case, U-C 63 was caught as she passed a well-known light-buoy north of the Dover Net Barrage. "E 52" (with her conning-tower only showing) attacked so as to keep the enemy against the moonlight. The only survivor was a Petty Officer, who gave the following account:—

The night being very cold, the Navigating Warrant Officer, who was on watch, sent the A.B. below to get some coffee. In the meantime the engineer of the boat came on the bridge and stood talking to the officer of the watch, who, in consequence, failed to keep a proper lookout. The Petty Officer himself, chancing to look to port, suddenly saw a submarine on the surface. . . . U-C 63 had just started to turn when she was struck by a torpedo amidships.

And that survivor's statement would be a good thing to frame and put on every ship's bridge in war-time! The critical time when a bad lookout was being kept could not have been more than a few seconds, but it was long enough to cause death to all but one of the submarine's crew.

The U-boats during the war torpedoed five of our boats, *viz.*: "E 3" in the Bight in August 1914, "E 20" in the Sea of Marmora in November 1915, "E 22" in April 1916 off Yarmouth, "C 34" off the Shetlands in July of 1917, and "D 6" in the Channel in June of 1918. Of these, "C 34" was hit when almost under— the German U 52 firing at the top of his conning-tower as it went down. "E 22" was attacked while beating up and down waiting for orders to proceed to any threatened area on the day of the Yarmouth raid. She saw U–B 18's periscope and tried to ram it, actually bending down the enemy's bow "net-cutters" (the big steel saw that stands up in the bows of U-boats). The German, however, passed under her and got his torpedo in as she turned back.

As far as is known, none of our boats were sunk by enemy submarines apart from the five named. On several occasions U-boats fired torpedoes and used guns against our boats, but the low hulls of English submarines provide very small targets. I suppose the majority of shells fired at English submarines came from English guns. Certainly the boats were far more nervous about approaching our own harbours than they were of working in enemy waters. The shooting was usually wild and could be treated as amusing, but on occasions fatal results precluded any joking.

The surface anti-submarine vessels drew no fine distinctions, and the submarines at times used to deplore their own side's excessive zeal. There is a short extract from a certain boat's signal-log which begins, "Can you give me my position?" and which continues, punctuated by nine rounds of gun-fire, by way of injured protests, to "What did you do in the Great War, Daddy?" as, her identity established and the patrol ship's attentions deflected, the submarine continued her way up harbour.

Out on the patrol areas, however, a British boat diving had to stand her chance. No surface ship could be expected to differentiate between our own and enemy periscopes, and the potency of British depth charges was highly spoken of by those of our boats that had experience of them.

CHAPTER 3

Watching for the Enemy Fleet

The work of the submarines on the anti-submarine patrols, mine-laying trips, etc., was useful, and at times exciting; but it must be remembered that the main duty of the flotillas lay in watching for the enemy's fleet, and that this duty continued throughout the war. Boats were stationed watching both the entrance to the Baltic and the several exits from the Bight right up to the date of the signing of the Armistice. For the first two years of the war the duty of these boats was to attack the enemy if seen, and to signal afterwards that the enemy had been met.

The signalling question then was a secondary consideration. The boats were considered less as scouts than as torpedo-boats, especially in view of the fact that in the early part of the war their wireless range was limited. When "E 23" (Lieutenant-Commander Turner) torpedoed the *Westfalen* in August 1916, he rose to the surface as the enemy drew out of sight and signalled the enemy's position to the commander-in-chief.

It is true that no decisive result came of the signal, as the enemy turned home when barely clear of the Bight, and the Grand Fleet's attempt to cut him off, as usually happened, failed again; but that signal was the first clear "enemy report" given by a unit of the Bight Patrol. It was then that new long-range wireless sets were installed in all boats, amid the curses of the submarine officers, who at that date were distinctly narrow-minded on the question of how their boats could be most usefully employed. They looked upon it as a personal insult that their limited accommodation should be cut down by the extra instruments supplied, and also that (this was where the shoe pinched) their splendid independence on patrol should be lost to them now that

Their lordships could call them up direct from the wireless at Whitehall. But they soon discovered that the idea was right, and that their loss of independence weighed nothing against the new strategic use which had been found for the submarine as a fleet scout. Orders were issued that the boats were on no account to fire at the enemy if he was seen coming out, until a wireless signal had been made to commander-in-chief. This, of course, implied that the boat could not attack the outward-bound High Sea Fleet at all, as the signal would have to be made from surface trim, and by the time it was acknowledged the chance of a torpedo attack would have gone by. If the enemy was seen homeward bound, the submarines were at liberty to fire at them; but outward-bound squadrons were safe from under-water attack. A submarine officer was heard to explain the reason for these orders by the light of his own logic:

"The commander-in-chief won't let us fire at them coming out, because he wants 'em for himself, and thinks if we butt in it discourages them and they lose their enthusiasm; I suppose he's right, but it looks a bit selfish. . . ."

During the last two years of the war, the enemy gradually discovered that such orders as these must have been given. The Naval Armistice Commission to Germany has heard some interesting sidelights on the war from the officers of the German Commission. A good deal of the information volunteered has to be left unconfirmed owing to the lack of opportunities for checking it, but in cases where it can be corroborated by our own information, it can be seen that the Germans see no object now in concealment or perversion of facts.

The following is from a German commander, a dignified solemn-featured figure standing rigidly on the bridge of an Allied destroyer, his face turned to the bank of the Kiel Canal that slid past him—a man who felt clearly the disgrace and humiliation that had come upon his country:—

We wondered why, when we made an excursion, we were not fired at. We knew you had submarines all round the Bight, and our ships even saw periscopes, but no torpedoes came. We thought after a while that it was an order—that we were being watched and reported, but left unmolested till the Grand Fleet should come. I remember when we came out one night and we heard the wireless speak by Hiorn's Reef. The operator heard it, but we could not block the signals. If we had blocked we would have been yet found—our position would have been known by the Directional Wireless in England.

We heard him sending by full power, and by the nature of his signal (it was so short and quick) we knew the purport of it. Then we went on, but all the time we knew it. We knew that we might meet the Fleet. It is impossible to leave the Bight without being reported. Then on the return by Hiorn's Reef the torpedo came and the *Moltke* was hit. She was badly damaged, but we towed her in. I do not know if it was the same submarine that saw us go out.

I do not think so. You do not know? No? It was perhaps the same, but you had many boats patrolling. The Zeppelins claimed many to be sunk with bombs. It was not so? No? The flying men are all full of imagination. It is the vibration of the engines that affects the eyes. . . .

. . . Yes, I was at the Skageraksclaght (the Jutland Battle). We were not hit. Some ships were badly hit. One ship [probably the *Seydlitz*—Author] had an artillery officer on board. It was his holiday, and he spent it on board her with his friend. He said after that he would prefer a year on the Western Front to twenty minutes' naval bombardment.

The doctors were all killed and the ship was on fire. The shells came into both casualty stations. Did many English ships receive hits from torpedoes? The *Marlborough* only?

That is strange, for we fired many. Yes, the Emperor said it was a victory, but if it had been a victory we would have known it without his having to tell us so. The sailors were not persuaded so. . . .

(I seem to be quoting irrelevant matter here, but German mentality at any rate bears on the submarine subject, even if indirectly.)

. . . The *Tiger* is not sunk? No? We thought not—we heard later that it was a dummy *Tiger* that was torpedoed. We were sure before that it was the real ship that sank, and the officer that fired was decorated. It is all right, because since then he has earned the decoration for other things, so that he does not mind. A lot of things we did not understand for long. Our submarines have seen your K-boats at sea. They saw them through the periscope, and could read the numbers, but they said they must be fast submarine-hunters, like the Americans were written to be building. Then one day a U-boat saw through his periscope a K-boat steaming, and then in one minute the K was submerged, so we knew it was really a submarine. What was the submarine that torpedoed the U 51 in the mouth of the Jahde river? That was a fine attack. The U-boat was not yet out of the river on its voyage. Did the English boat get home? Yes. I am glad—she had many depth-charges to face.

Your mine-laying submarines were dangerous. They had a trick of following our mine-sweeping boats up the channel. They did not lay mines until the channel was swept and reported free. It was well organised . . . and also the submarine that struck the mine and yet got back. The captain of her is to be congratulated; we heard of it and we thought she was very lucky—I think it was at Amrum bank she struck the mine. I think it was an English mine; one of our mines would have put her in pieces. I do not know why the Heligoland trawlers did not see her as she was passing home to England. . . .

I must just hark back to the question of the U-boat here, as the Inspection Commissions in Germany that are seeing to the handing over or destruction of the U-boats bring back their reports here, and their reports are full of interest, though perhaps they contain little that is news to the Admiralty. There are now 135 German submarines in England, and there are more to come yet. The building-yards of Germany show that a huge effort was to have been made along the lines of submarine war in the spring and summer of 1919.

Every available yard was working at full power at the date of the cessation of hostilities, and the work was almost entirely on submarine construction. The only other work being done was on new and more powerful destroyers and on standard merchant ships—the latter for after-the-war reconstruction. Yards that had never before done warship work of any kind were fully employed on building small submarines. The big yards were given all the new submarine-cruiser work to do. The submarine cruisers were a comparative failure on trials, as were also the big submarine mine-layers of the U 118 class; this must have been a sad disappointment to the enemy, as one can judge by the number of big boats preparing that he had set his heart on a campaign of thorough frightfulness on the American coast in the spring.

Work on the new big surface ships had stopped in the spring of 1918, partly owing to the shortage of nickel and chiefly owing to their whole stake having been put on submarines and not on the Fleet. The German mentality never seems to have grasped the fundamental rule of sea-fighting—that commerce-destruction will never win a war, and that only the defeat or mastery of the main enemy fleet can bring command of the sea.

Such yards as the two at Hamburg (Vulcan and Blohm & Voss) are typical of the method of construction. On November 11 these two yards had seventy-two submarines under construction. At the same time at Blohm & Voss's yard the battle-cruiser *Mackensen* lay abandoned in the water just as she had been launched in the spring of 1918, and the battleship *Ersatz Freya* lay half-finished on the building-slip. The submarines were on the slips in rows—each row representing a group or perhaps seven boats of the same class.

Lying alongside each row were parts and fittings waiting to be built in: for instance, seven bows (complete with sterns and torpedo-tube pads), seven sterns (complete with hydroplane-guards, etc.), seven bow top-strakes, seven stern top-strakes, etc.—in fact, one was reminded strongly of what one had heard of American motor-car factories. The whole idea was of quick and standardised production, and the two points that occurred at once to the observer were—"There would have been a deuce of a rush of new stuff into commission in the spring," and then, "How on earth were they going to provide skilled crews for such a lot of boats all at once?"

The latter question is still difficult to answer, even if one takes into account a system of "compulsory volunteering," and also the fact that standardised boats can be worked by standard-ised and partly-trained men. What it would have come to was indicated by the trend of U-boat war results in 1918. It would have implied a good deal of real work being performed by a few experienced and trained crews, and a lot of blank trips and half-hearted performances by a mass of other crews, the mortal-ity among the latter rising to a terrible percentage. It will always be the same; a good personnel will do well in any boat—a bad personnel will do badly, however good the boat is.

In the remarks quoted from a German officer, I have referred to three incidents in connection with the activities of our own submarines. I will give them in their order, as they appeared to the officers concerned. It was "E 42" (Lieutenant C. Allen) that met the German battle-cruisers on 25th April 1918, and, the enemy being homeward bound, fired a torpedo into the *Moltke* as she passed Hiorn's Reef:—

a.m. 0630. While on surface, sighted hostile sea-plane—high up, but close.
Dived to 60 feet (4 bombs). Surfaced for observations. Saw

58

smoke bearing N.E. Dived.

Sighted a battle-cruiser escorted by three torpedo-boats. Altered course, and proceeded utmost speed to attack. Fired starboard bow tube (quarter shot). Range 2000-2500 yards. Heard sound of explosion a long way off—possible hit."

(The "possible hit," as a matter of fact, caused the *Moltke* to be towed in a very precarious condition all the way home.)

About five depth-charges and twenty lance-bombs were dropped at me after the shot. Courses as requisite for getting clear.

The next incident, of the attack in the Weser river, has a story behind it.

Lieutenant Varley ("H 5") reports as follows:—

11th July 1916: Fixed by Terschelling Light. Proceeded towards Ems." (*At this moment "H 5," being bored with the patrol billet assigned to her, and thirsting for trouble, left her patrol to see what was going on in Germany.—Author.*)

12th July, 2 a.m.: Dived off Borkum. 10.25 p.m.: dived to avoid destroyer. 10.50: surface, proceeding east, sighted enemy patrol vessel, but steamed round her without being seen.

13th July, 1 a.m.: Sighted Wangeroog and Rote Land Lights. 9.58 p.m.: sighted destroyer about 2 miles N.W. from Aussen Jahde Lightship.

14th July, 12.34 a.m.: Dived— several destroyers of G 101 class in sight. Attacked same. 10 a.m.: sighted hostile submarine—attacked same. Torpedoed submarine with one torpedo amidship. Surface to look for survivors. Was put down immediately by destroyer, who opened fire. 10.41: altered course N., and went to bottom in 18 fathoms. Heard loud explosion. Destroyers sweeping for us all day. During my attack there was just enough sea to make depth-keeping difficult. I fired two torpedoes, allowing 10 knots speed. One torpedo hit just before conning tower. Previous to this, on the 12th, the periscope had become very stiff to turn, and would not lower as far as the jumping-wire. During dark hours I endeavoured to rectify same, but while doing so was forced to dive, and so lost all the tools and parts of the centre bush, which left the periscope in the same condition throughout the trip.

While attacking, it took two men besides myself to turn the periscope. For this reason I did not think it advisable to attack the destroyers after having sunk the submarine. After torpedoing submarine, I proceeded four miles north, and lay on the bottom in eighteen fathoms. Many vessels were heard in close proximity. Several explosions, one very heavy one. On one occasion a sweep-wire scraped the whole length of the boat along the port side, and a vessel was heard to pass directly overhead.

I very much regret to report my slight transgression from orders. ...

The Navy, however, takes no cognisance of zeal, if misplaced. There is a story of a sailor of the Napoleonic wars who took a fort from the French single-handed. The resultant row with his commanding officer, who had been waiting some hours with all his men drawn up in order to carry out that identical duty in due military form, caused him to remark that "He'd never take another fort for them as long as he lived." The captain of the *Maidstone*, as is the way of the Service, shielded his subordinate from the wrath of My Lords, who were naturally aghast at an officer having left his assigned patrol area; but having taken the responsibility for the fault of his bull-terrier, he proceeded to lay into him thoroughly himself, while commenting publicly as follows:—

Lieutenant Varley is a very able and gallant sub-marine officer, and although there is no possible excuse for his having disregarded his orders and proceeded to the Weser, it is submitted that his skilful and successful attack on the German submarine, in spite of a defective periscope, and his subsequent conduct, especially during the critical time when he was being swept for by destroyers with explosive sweeps, may be taken into consideration.

It was, however, a year before Lieutenant Varley was decorated for this action, My Lords deciding that after that interval the example he had created would be forgotten.

I have mentioned the question of our own boats' experiences of depth-charges. A few instances of both English and German anti-submarine strafing may be of interest. At the beginning of the war the German depth-charge was a thing of contempt, and its English counterpart was nearly as useless. Submarines were sunk in those days by what might be called "accidental" methods. The boat either made a mistake and was then rammed or destroyed by gunfire, or else it met a mine or ran into nets. Depth-charges were not big enough to be dangerous, and it was not realised that even a big depth-charge must explode very close to the boat's hull before actual damage is caused.

Moral effect is, of course, a different thing: there is a case of a U-boat surrendering as a result of one rivet having been knocked out of her hull by a comparatively distant explosion. That, of course, is a matter of personnel; and the depth-charges we used often had a remarkable effect, although no structural damage whatever had been caused by them. When our big depth-charges were first supplied, patrol boats and destroyers carried but few of them and were expected to be sparing in their use—in fact, they were not supposed to use them unless a fair chance was seen of an almost direct hit.

Later, in 1917, the supply exceeded the demand—at least the demand on the previous scale—and anti-submarine vessels were supplied with just as many as they could comfortably stow on their decks; while orders were issued that any patch of water in which there was the faintest possibility or suspicion of a U-boat being present was to be sprinkled with depth-charges until there was no possibility of anything intact remaining in range. It is a feature of life in submarines that one always gives the hunters credit for seeing more than they do see: one watches a Zeppelin through the periscope—a Zeppelin cruising at perhaps five miles' range away—and one feels a sort of shrinking and an inclination to slip down to ninety feet or so for a spell in the certainty that one's periscope must have been seen.

Of course it hasn't, and it probably won't be. One meets a dark shape at night, and one does a "crash dive" at once, heaving a sigh of relief as one sees the gauge show sixty feet. One forgets that a submarine, besides being a much smaller mark to see at night, keeps in all probability a far better look-out than any other class of vessel. In the same way, the explosion of a depth-charge usually sounds closer than it is, and the submarine officer is inclined to jump to the conclusion that it is directly aimed at him or at some indication of his wake. As a matter of fact it is more probably aimed at an oil-patch or a piece of drift-wood some half-mile off, and the ship dropping it has no real knowledge of the submarine's proximity at all.

One German U-boat officer stated that in his last five trips he had heard an average of 150 charges per trip exploded in his vicinity. It is probable that only a small percentage of these were dropped on clear knowledge of his presence. Being an officer of good morale this profusion had not worried him, but with a less experienced captain some direct results would probably have been gained.

In the notes taken from the conversation of the German officers, the case of the English boat that met a mine at Amrum Bank is mentioned. The case provides a good illustration of what a direct hit, even by a full-sized mine, will not do, when the morale of officers and men is of the ideal standard, which every submarine service tries to obtain.

(I keep referring to "English boats"; in this case I mean by that that the captain was Canadian, and most of the rest of the crew Scotch or Colonial.) The report is written by the captain of the *Maidstone*.

Submarine 'H 8' (Lieutenant-Commander B. L. Johnson,

R.N.R.), when diving at 60 ft. off Ameland Gat on March 22, 1916, heard a slight scraping noise forward, which was followed by a violent explosion. The submarine immediately sank by the bows and struck the bottom at 85 ft. with an inclination of 25° or 30°. . . .

The captain reports that although it appeared obvious to all that the boat was lost, the officers and entire crew proceeded to their stations without any sign of excitement, and all orders were carried out promptly and correctly. I would submit that such conduct, in the face of apparent certain death, is an example of which the whole Service may be proud.

Motors were put to full speed astern, and Nos. 2 and 3 ballast-tanks were blown—No. 1 being found open to the sea. The submarine then came to the surface. Fuel was then blown, and after some temporary repairs had been made, course was shaped for Terschelling, and then Harwich.

The damage to 'H 8' is serious, the mine having exploded against the starboard forward hydroplane. Both forward hydroplanes and the bow cap are gone; the upper part of the hull in that vicinity as well as both starboard torpedo-tubes are wrecked. All bulkheads appear to be strained, but luckily the one near the rear of the torpedo-tubes, although leaking, did not give way. . . .

This boat came out of the Bight and back to Harwich at slow speed on the surface and with a large part of her forward buoyancy destroyed. The luck that watches over the competent took her back unmolested by the enemy. There is a case where the run back of a damaged boat was performed over a yet greater distance through enemy waters.

On the 21st June 1915 submarine "S 1" (Lieutenant-Commander Kellett) was ten miles north of Heligoland. She dived during the day on several occasions, owing to sighting one Zeppelin, one seaplane, nineteen trawlers (sweeping in lines), and she also attacked, fired at, and missed a destroyer. Her port engine then broke down completely. On the 22nd, by Hiorn's Reef Light-vessel, she sighted a Zeppelin and a Parseval. She worked on engine defects all day while diving.

On the 23rd the starboard engine broke down completely, and she continued to work on defects. A Zeppelin was in sight nearly all day. On the 24th she captured the German trawler *Ost*. She put a prize crew of five hands with Lieutenant Kennedy on board, passed a tow-rope over, and started back to Yarmouth. On the 25th the trawler's engine broke down. "S 1's" crew refitted the HP piston, crossheads and crankhead bearings, and at four knots speed the strange procession proceeded on out of the Bight. On the 26th they stopped to refit the trawler's L.P. cylinder (they must have been by this time thoroughly sick and tired of engines and all to do with them), and proceeded. On the 27th June they made a triumphant arrival.

There seems to be a special providence that watches over people who won't admit defeat. I don't know about faith moving mountains, but (I'm sorry to have to use the word, but my vocabulary is limited) it was "guts" that brought "H 8" and "S 1" home safely.

Getting back to the question of depth-charges—one may pass over the little explosive sweep-charges used by the Germans early in the war. They were more like squibs than anything else. The Zeppelin bombs were noisy, but burst on the surface only, and so were innocuous to a boat below 30 or 40 feet depth. Later on, in 1917, the Germans began to use depth-charges in their destroyers and patrol boats; but these weapons were not only too light for useful results to be expected from them, but were also dropped too vaguely and inaccurately for our boats to have much respect for them.

I will quote some recent cases which refer to the best depth-charges the enemy produced during the war:—

Midnight, *Oct. 2nd*, 1918; 'L 15' (Lieutenant-Commander Ward): Vessel, apparently T.B.D., appeared suddenly on port beam, distant 100 yards. Dived to 60 feet. Vessel passed overhead (turbine engine). Heard two loud explosions in quick succession."

7.45 a.m., *March 24th*, 1918; 'E 44' (Lieutenant Venning):
Five battleships (apparently of *Kaiser* class) and a destroyer
(the latter zigzagging). Turned to attack on surface. The
destroyer turned towards me and fired a white Very's light.
His range was about 2000 and the big ships 4000 yards. All
ships then altered course. 7.50 a.m.: dived at full speed. Hit
bottom hard at 64 feet, and proceeded along bottom at
full speed. 7.53: one depth-charge exploded astern. 7.55:
another depth-charge exploded astern. I stopped engines.
8.5 a.m.: went ahead 6 knots. 8.10: destroyer passed overhead, and the sweep-wire was heard scraping over the
'jumping wire.' 9.30 a.m.: eased to four knots. Sounds of
propellers died away. Under-water explosions were heard
at intervals till 11 a.m.

If this chance had been given, in such shoal water, to a British
destroyer screen, the submarine would certainly not have been
so calm about it.

There are some first-hand reports on our own depth-charges:—

Submarine "D 7," February 10th, 1918 (Lieutenant Tweedy),
suddenly sighted H.M.S. *Pelican* through her periscope. She increased to full speed and went down deeper, altering course
from north to west.

3.48 p.m.: First explosion occurred, loud and violent, but
no damage or inconvenience. Very shortly after-wards a
second explosion. This was considerably more violent,
shattering several lights and flooding the after-periscope.
Heavy shock throughout the boat, but no serious damage.
Order was given to 'blow externals.' While rising, a third
explosion occurred of about the same intensity as the first.
On breaking surface made recognition signals. . . .

The comment of authority on the incident blandly points
out that by more accurate judging of speeds, distances, etc., the

estimated distance of 150 yards between "D 7" and the second depth-charge could have been much reduced and better results obtained. There is, of course, no hint that the destroyer was to blame in the matter of recognition. In all these cases it is the destroyer's duty to take it for granted that any periscope is hostile, and the comments on these reports usually show some sympathy with the surface ship's natural disappointment at finding she has attacked one of her own side.

On 29th Feb. 1918, submarine "L 2" (Lieutenant-Commander Acworth) had a similar experience, which had very little that was amusing about it. Her opponents were the United States' destroyers *Paulding, Davis*, and *Trippe*.

> . . . I lowered periscope and dived to 90 feet. Gunshots being heard, I proceeded at full speed to 200 feet, at which depth the first heavy depth-charge exploded, and at the same time the after-hydroplanes jammed hard-up. We now took a tremendous inclination by the stern, the tail touching the bottom at 300 feet.
>
> "Four more very heavy explosions shook the boat. Bright flashes were seen in the boat, and she was at an angle of 45°, bow up. We were unable to correct this trim with the forward hydroplanes, so I gave the order to blow Nos. 5 and 6. This order was promptly obeyed, and the boat slowly commenced to rise, but at a tremendous angle. On breaking surface three destroyers opened a hot fire on us at a range of 1000 yards—one shot striking the pressure-hull just abaft the conning-tower. Recognition signals were made, and White Ensign waved, when firing ceased.

The American destroyers had sighted the top of the conning-tower of "L 2" as she "broke surface," diving in the rough swell. The submarine authorities comment on the incident as follows:

> In view of the small amount of conning-tower exposed and the distance at which it was sighted, it is submitted that these vessels made a most remarkably efficient attack.

It is curious that both British and German submarine officers have the same opinion of aircraft as anti-submarine weapons. Our boats looked on Zeppelins as scouts only—as bombers they could be practically neglected. The German seaplanes became dangerous towards the end of the war from the fact that they carried machine-guns: their bombs were trifling affairs. But any aircraft might locate a boat on patrol, and then the boat might just as well not be there, because no target worth a torpedo would be foolish enough to come within range of her, once the warning had been given.

Similarly, the Germans stated that what they disliked most in the Irish Sea were the airships and seaplanes that were always passing over them. They did not fear the bombs these craft carried, but they did dislike having their own position continually reported to the surface patrols, who, as a result, gave them little rest. There is no doubt that the morale of submarine personnel is much affected by continual nerve-strain. For a man to be able to keep up a long patrol and retain his full faculties he must have some part of the day or night free from worry, even if it is only a couple of hours during which he may feel safe from aggression. In the Heligoland Bight it was a tremendous relief to be able, at the end of a harassing day, to sink to the bottom and retire from the war for a few hours.

The sense of relief and relaxation was extraordinarily grateful. It must be remembered that, even if nothing is in sight through the periscope, the officers and crew have still at the back of their minds the recollection of the number of boats which have been lost, presumably by mines, in the Bight, and of whose fate no explanation has ever been forthcoming. If a submarine can be given no rest, day or night, from the ever-present fear of death, she is soon in a state when over-tired nerves will infallibly commit some mistake which will make her an easier victim.

In this connection aircraft may be described as an infernal nuisance. You never can be certain if they have seen you or not, and the tendency is to take it for granted that they have done so. If you are then in enemy waters you must be on the *qui vive* for being hunted by the usual methods; if not in actual enemy local waters, you feel that your chance of a target has gone for the day, and that even if a target does come by, she will be well protected and on the look-out for periscopes. On the whole, however, the German aircraft did not do much, and they certainly did not make the British submarines nervous.

The game, in fact, rather worked the other way, as far as the Zeppelins were concerned. It was easy to work out (the German being of a methodical and regular nature), from the continued reports of our boats of the times and rendezvous of Zeppelin patrols, just where a Zeppelin might be expected to be found, and the resultant action by our own aircraft brought two of these huge sea-scouts down in flames. It should be mentioned that our boats are supplied with "sky-searcher" periscopes, which can either sweep the horizon or swivel so as to watch the motions of anything from the horizontal plane up to the zenith.

A seaplane is a different proposition. Submarine "C 25" was attacked by five German seaplanes off Harwich on 6th July 1918. Several thousand rounds of machine-gun ammunition were fired at her and a number of bombs dropped. The bombs, even when they hit direct, did very little damage, being of probably not more than 10 lb. weight. The incendiary bullets from the machine-guns, however, killed the captain (Lieutenant Bell) and five men, who from a position on the bridge were trying to drive off the enemy with a Lewis gun.

As the incident occurred close to the English coast, the success of the enemy on this occasion may be put down to the fact that the submarine, under the impression that the aircraft must be friendly, made no attempt to dive until the bursting of a couple of bombs on her hull rendered her incapable of submerging.

Seaplanes have the advantage of attack in that they are able, on sighting a submarine on the surface, to come down volplane from the clouds, the first intimation of their presence being given by the roar of their engines as they level off close alongside. Submarine "E 4" was nearly caught in this way once near Hiorn's Reef. She had just come to the surface for a look round and to get latitude observations. Lieutenant-Commander Julian Tenison, her captain, was sitting comfortably on the bridge-rail while the tanks were being blown below in order to give the boat convenient buoyancy. The seaplane had dived down on him in the path of the sun, and the rip r.r.rip-room of the switched-on engines 200 yards away brought Tenison to his feet with a jump.

He realised instantly that there was no time to get under before the enemy could let go his bombs—the change from blowing to flooding tanks would take far more than the usual 30 seconds which suffices to submerge a boat under normal conditions. He reached down, pressed the button of the "diving-hooter," and then stood up and enthusiastically waved his cap to the seaplane pilot. The pilot shot past at a few yards' range, giving a half-hearted wave in return, as a man responds to a perfect stranger who salutes him in the street.

As the machine passed, Tenison jumped down below and pulled the lid to: the short delay had been enough for the blows to be shut off and the vents to be thrown open, and the boat was starting under. Through the periscope, before the hull was down, he saw the machine turn ahead of him, coming round on a wing-tip, and evidently now fully awake to the situation. The boat drove under, and at eighteen feet three bombs burst on the surface in quick succession over the forepart of the hull. Being the usual small bombs no damage was done, but had they struck the hull while it was still above water the chances for "E 4" would have been poor. It is quite possible that the German pilot has not to this day seen anything amusing in the incident.

Although Zeppelins did not, as far as is known, cause our submarines any damage by bombing or other aggressive action, they were a great nuisance, in that they often caused delay to the boats on passage to their areas. One had to dive in order to avoid being reported; and it was aggravating to be kept under by a great silver brute which appeared to have nothing better to do than to cruise aimlessly round in a five-mile circle overhead. It was therefore a great relief when a chance occurred for a boat to get her own back and square accounts a little. On the 9th May 1916, at 9.30 a.m., "E 31" (Lieutenant -Commander Fielman) observed a Zeppelin in difficulties, apparently sinking towards the water.

The airship was "L 7," which had been under fire, and had received damage from our light-cruiser forces. She settled down till the gondolas touched, and started to "taxi" towards home. "E 31" rose ahead of her and opened fire with a bow gun. On the third hit the Zeppelin burst into flames, and disappeared in thirty seconds or so. Seven survivors were picked up, and "E 31" dived again and proceeded on towards Harwich. At midnight a German four-funnelled cruiser was seen coming right at them, and barely 200 yards away on the starboard bow. Lieutenant Love, R.N.R., officer of the watch, acted swiftly.

He put the helm hard a-starboard and rang the diving alarm. The cruiser was pretty smart in her actions also. She ported her helm to ram; but "E 31," being inside her turning circle, was missed by fifty yards. As she passed, she switched on searchlights and opened "independent fire" (i e. "fire as fast as you can and as often as possible at whatever you can see of the target"). One 5·9 shell hit the submarine's forward superstructure two feet above the hull, but did not explode. As the gauge reached sixty feet, "E 31" heard the cruiser pass overhead. It is understood that the seven Zeppelin prisoners observed, as the boat levelled off at the bottom to wait for quieter times overhead, that it was a rotten war anyway, and that they would be glad when it was over.

One thing which the submarine service in war-time seems to engender, is extraordinary impudence towards the enemy. This state of mind is based partly on contempt and partly on complete confidence in one's crew and boat. At the beginning of the war it was a marked feature in the work of our boats; but later on, when the watching patrol was established, things had to be taken more seriously, because it was inadvisable for the presence of boats in the patrol areas to be known of by the enemy.

There are several instances which will illustrate the mental attitude of our officers towards their foes before the patrol-ring was formally established round the Bight. I would instance "E 5" (Lieutenant-Commander Benning), who, on the 16th August 1915, seeing a German destroyer about four miles off, near the mouth of the Elbe, came to the surface and opened the conning-tower hatch "to attract her." The attraction was apparently sufficient, as the destroyer charged at full speed. "E 5" dived, turned outwards, and then, swinging in again, fired a torpedo as the enemy rushed past. The destroyer, the sea being very smooth, saw the firing-splash, and, by putting her helm hard a-port, dodged the torpedo. She then ceased to be "attracted," and departed hurriedly.

The island of Heligoland has been a wonderful source of inspiration to the newspapers throughout the war. It has been described as being the strategic pivot of the North Sea, and as the heavily-fortified base of the High Sea Fleet. The importance of the place may be better gauged if it is explained that it has just about the fighting value that an old battleship would have if moored out head and stern on the shoal, but with the disadvantage of the guns being unable to obtain "all-round" training.

The harbour has only enough depth of water for trawlers and torpedo-boats; the High Sea Fleet couldn't get in if it wished to. If we had had possession of it instead of the enemy, we would have lost heavily in trying to keep it. Our position there would have been rather as if the Germans had tried to hold the Ship-wash Light-vessel off Harwich; it would have been too exciting for words. At any rate Heligoland is not a submarine base, and as long as there are far better bases on the mainland, it is not likely to be used for that purpose. I have heard it stated that U-boats use the island as an "advanced port" which allowed them to shorten their journeys out on patrol. Such use of the island would shorten a voyage by some thirty miles, but when the voyage implies a mileage of perhaps 6000, a matter of thirty is hardly worth noticing.

From our submarines' point of view the place was useful to take bearings of and to fix position on, and except for navigational purposes they took little interest in it,—so little, in fact, that "E 2" (Lieutenant -Commander Stocks), when she ran aground there, barely referred to the incident in her log. Submarines are delightful things to navigate in. A surface ship has a certain fixed draught, and she has to keep that figure always before her mind's eye. A submarine never approaches the coast or navigates in thick weather, unless trimmed down until she is drawing several feet more than usual.

When in this condition a meeting with the shore does not matter much. If she slides up on the land, she blows her tanks and slides off again, so that grounding in a submarine comes to be looked on as a very ordinary and matter-of-fact sort of business. "E 2" was cruising in a fog in the Bight, and was trimmed down in case of accidents, when she came well on to the beach under the western cliffs of Heligoland,—she was so close to the gun-emplacement that the guns could not be depressed enough to bear on her, which was certainly fortunate.

The Germans were very agitated. They ran about, hailing and bellowing at her and working themselves up to a great state of mind. "E 2," however, blew her tanks out and backed off; as she did so a torpedo-boat arrived and opened fire on her. "E 2," finding salvos falling close aboard of her, decided that there was hardly time to turn round and depart submerged in the usual way, so she continued to go astern, and, reversing the hydroplanes, dived off backwards—none of the shots hitting her; and, in fact, the accurate estimation of deflection by the torpedo-boat, in view of "E 2's" squid-like action, must have been difficult.

A matter that caused a good deal of amusement to our submarine service throughout the war, and which probably made the Germans laugh also, was the great "petrol myth." It is a story which is at least as good as the Russian troops that travelled through England. Every part of the coast was reported to be the scene of mysterious rendezvous between U-boats and German spies, and at these meetings petrol cans changed hands—the U-boats taking the full tins, and the spy, presumably, insisting on getting the empty tins back, or else the sum of two shillings each in lieu. Heaven knows who invented the story, but it sounds like a "leg-pull," which had got out of hand and spread like a disease. For one thing, submarines don't use petrol—they use Diesel engines and heavy oil. For another thing, a submarine, depending on her size, carries from 30 to 300 tons of fuel in her tanks.

If a wicked German spy was kind enough to take a couple of tins of petrol aboard a U-boat, he would, presuming that the captain owned a motor bicycle, be gladly welcomed; but his gift would hardly add to the radius of action of the boat. A submarine can keep the sea longer than a surface ship can, and has a much longer radius of action—the heavy-oil engine is economical and efficient, and such things as special fuel-carrying tenders or submerged fuel-tanks are unnecessary luxuries.

It is true that U-boats used on occasions the little creeks and bays of Scotland and the Orkneys to shelter in, and in fact one boat landed some men on one of the smaller Orkney islands and stole half a dozen sheep; but such exploits are more matters of amusement than business. Our boats in the Bight used to shoot duck occasionally (and the Frisian Islands are a paradise for wild-fowl shooters in January—the birds are to be seen in thousands at a time), and if there had been anything else worth stealing on the very uninviting and ugly German coast, I'm certain that nothing but the innate honesty of our submarine officers would have prevented them from getting it.

As for the German spy scares, the Germans had a similar experience at the beginning of the war. Quite a number of perfectly good Huns were shot by enthusiastic amateur sentries, and the patriotic citizen felt it a duty to let off what firearms he had at any car which drove fast after dark, or which showed strong lights. The rumours of communication between U-boats and spies on the coasts of Great Britain continued throughout the war, while all the time the real German spies continued to send their reports by letters, and the N.I.D. continued to open the letters and substitute their own versions of the news.

The fact is, very little information got away to Germany except through the newspapers. This country has the disadvantage, from an enemy spy's point of view, of being an island; Germany has a neutral country on each side of her: as a result, when the Armistice came, the Germans could give us little news about their Navy—everything of interest about it was already known at our Admiralty. There were some other widely believed "facts" about submarines which are dying a very slow death. They mostly came from the brains of the Press naval correspondents.

One was that a submarine could not keep the sea more than a day or two. Of course, long before the war, even our little C-class boats were spending ten days on manoeuvres. The first long trip of the war was "E 11's" thirty-one days in the Sea of Marmora. Again, it was solemnly proved when the *Hogue*, Cressy, and *Aboukir* were sunk, that more than one U-boat must have been present, "as a submarine cannot reload under water."

I am mentioning these things, as it has been a matter of surprise to the submarine services of all navies that the boats have been looked on as new arrivals, and as weapons which were completely new and untried in 1914. The fact is, the submarine "arrived" long before the war, and has been used in annual manoeuvres in our Navy since 1904. The first successful submarine attack, it should be noted, was by the Confederate submersible which sank the *Housatonic* in the American Civil War—some fifty-seven years ago.

There is no doubt that the German submarine service had everything in its favour.

They had targets in plenty, in view of the fact that our fleet kept the sea practically continuously at the beginning of the war, and for about 25 *per cent*, of the time during the later stages. The coasts of these islands are ideal for submarines to work round; the shore is mostly steep-to, and the high landmarks make navigation easy. The German coast is low and difficult to see; it is guarded by outlying shoals and islands, and the visibility offshore is usually poor; the numerous rivers emptying into the Bight make diving conditions bad at times owing to the alternate strata formed of fresh and salt water.

Altogether, the two sets of conditions used to make our submarine service often wish that the two belligerent navies might change fleets, bases, and strategic problems, and so give our boats a chance to show how a weaker navy should carry out a war of attrition. Such a war could undoubtedly have been fought very much more efficiently by the enemy if he had concentrated on warship-targets only.

There is a clause in a German instructional book for submarine officers which directs the young idea to "never attack a man-of-war if there is chance of usefully attacking commerce" (or words to that effect). That sort of order is an admission of defeat, as although the axiom, that "the object of strategy is the defeat of the main forces of the enemy," was, I believe, laid down by Napoleon, it is as old as the time of the first battle between tribes of Palaeolithic men. A defeat of the Grand Fleet by direct naval action would have given Germany domination of the world; but the works of the late Admiral Mahan do not seem to have been understood in Berlin.

The great German commerce-destroying submarine navy is now no more. Its fate will be a reminder to strategists of the future that a *guerre de course* never won a war yet, and that there is no easy road to victory. It may be easier "to attack merchant ships rather than men-of-war," but if the result is the surrender of one's own Navy, the policy seems hardly profitable.

However, our own submarine strategy was, in spite of the enemy's example, kept on correct lines; our leaders saw the possibilities and the future of this type of craft far more clearly than did Admiral Tirpitz. Our boats were built and used for military purposes only, and their work was all part of the main strategical policy of the Navy.

CHAPTER 4

Submarines, Sailors & Seaplanes

1

Facing each other across the southern part of the North Sea were the opposing submarine bases of Harwich and Flanders. The boats from these bases occasionally met and fought, but in the main their duties lay well apart. Harwich boats worked off the Bight, while the Flanders ports were bases for U-boats to start from on their way down channel to the traffic routes. The losses of the Flanders boats were heavy—so were the losses of the 8th Flotilla at Harwich, especially in 1916.

In that year the 8th Flotilla submarine officers passed a self-denying ordinance to reduce their consumption of alcohol. (Now what I am leading up to is a comparison of British and German mentality, because I think the question of personnel to be infinitely more important than that of material.) The fact is, that heavy losses do affect those who are left to carry on the work. A boat comes back to harbour with her officers and crew tired and glad to be home again; they are perhaps met with, "Did you see anything of Seventy-six? He's been overdue three days. He was next to you—off Ameland. You didn't hear anything go up? Oh, well, you'll probably have that billet next week and you may find out. . . ."

Well, it does affect people, and there is undoubtedly a great feeling of relief at getting back to harbour safely. In the Navy, where wines and spirits are free of duty, alcohol is cheap and obtainable, and alcohol is a relief from worry and an opiate for tired nerves. But the war has never seen a case of disciplinary action being necessary to control our submarine officers. It is a difficult question to approach in print, as the temperance argument seems to call out such strongly-expressed opinions from the advocates pro and con; but while I have no idea of holding up submarine officers as paragons of abstinence (for I hardly know any who are teetotallers), there is no doubt that they fully realised that only moderation could keep them efficient for war.

Over in Flanders it was the rule for U-boats to base at Bruges, and to use only Ostend and Zeebrugge as they passed through on their way to and from the sea. At Bruges the U-boat officers had a mess at the house of M. Catulle—a large, well-furnished, and comfortable building near the docks. There the officers had made the cellars (three inter-connected vaults) into an underground Rest for Tired Workers. All around the walls are painted frescoes illustrating the minds of the patrons.

The frescoes are over two feet in depth, and are well executed in the type of German humour one meets in the Berlin comic papers. There are mines, projectiles, etc., with the conventional faces and hats of John Bull, France, and other Allies; dancing with the mines are torpedoes, some of which carry on them the faces of dead U-boat officers. Beneath the frescoes are mottoes—such as, *Drink, for tomorrow you may die—Life is short, and you'll be a long time dead*. Between the pictures are smaller paintings of monkeys drinking champagne.

After dinner, according to witnesses, the officers would retire to these cellars and drink. There is little ventilation, and the atmosphere must have been fairly thick with smoke and fumes. Drinking some-times continued till 8 a.m.—a horrible hour at which to be drunk. It is reported by Belgians that the officers got through four thousand bottles of wine in three weeks. Taking the high estimate of an average of twenty officers always present, this means ten bottles per head a day—which is absurd. It is probable, however, that the competitors broke or gave away a good many bottles.

But there is no doubt they went at it pretty fast; one officer was drunk and incapable for five days on end, and (as apparently there was considered to be a limit of four days for states of coma) on the fifth day was ordered to sea by the captain of the Flotilla "to cool his head." The whole impression one gets from the local stories is one of fear, morbid excitement, and drink.

The pictures conjured up are unpleasant: the early morning scene in the cellars when a few hiccoughing stalwarts still sat over their wine—the guttural attempt at song—the pale glow of electric lamps through swirling smoke—the reek of alcohol—the litter of bottles—and the frightened face of the Belgian chambermaid peering round the angle of the cellar stairs. "Karl and Schmidt have not returned—God punish the English! Open more bottles, fool, and let us forget that our turn is coming!"

How the flotillas were able to do efficient work at all is a puzzle; but the Flanders Flotillas did the Allies a lot of harm. Had it not been the custom of the officers to throw off restraint in harbour, we might have suffered a good deal more—how much more only a student of psychology can guess. But there is no doubt of this—and a comparison of the Harwich and Flanders Flotillas shows it—the British take to games to soothe their nerves and the Germans to drink.

It is possibly something to do with this trait that brought the major part of the U-boat successes into the hands of a few special officers. The greater part of the captains did little; a few "aces" compiled huge lists of sunken tonnage to their credit (or otherwise). Judged by British Admiralty standards of efficiency, those few are the only ones who in our Service would have been retained at all.

However, it is time I went on with the doings of our own boats. Human beings are so much more important in war than are machines, that it is a temptation to describe them for preference. I would like to be able to talk about the submarine seamen also, but there is no ground for comparison between our own men and the German machine-made U-boat hand. One thinks of the German men as just things that opened or closed valves when barked at, and who never took any interest in what was going on outside their particular stations, or in what the boat was doing. Our sailors are—well, to put it "socially," they seem to belong more to the middle than the lower class. They are certainly not machine-made or dull, and they are not reluctant to act according to their own judgment in the absence of an officer's orders.

During the war our submarines sank 54 enemy warships and 274 other vessels. These figures do not, of course, include the many warships which were damaged but which were got back into harbour, although they include the U-boats which our submarines destroyed. German ships are very well subdivided in compartments and take a lot of killing. Certainly on a modern war-vessel one torpedo-hit is very little use; it takes about four to make certain of sinking her. The *Moltke* (battle-cruiser) was hit with one torpedo forward in the Baltic by Commander Laurence, and again off Hiorn's Reef by Lieutenant Allen (right aft this time); on each occasion she got home safely. Our own light cruiser *Falmouth* had to receive four torpedoes in succession before she sank.

The *Prinz Adalbert* was torpedoed by Commander Horton in the Baltic off Cape Kola and returned safely to Kiel (she could not take a hint, however, and after a long interval for repair she went east again and met Commander Goodheart of "E 8," who sank her). Commander Laurence in "J 1" hit the *Kronprinz* and *Grosser Kurfurst* (battleships) in the North Sea, but both were got home safely. Our later submarines were fitted with larger torpedoes and tubes, but the boats fitted with eighteen-inch torpedoes made up the larger part of our flotillas, and it was realised by both our own and the enemy submarines that it took several hits with the smaller-size weapon to finish off a large ship.

Perhaps the clearest case on record is that of the *Marlborough*, the ship being hit by a torpedo at the Jutland battle and remaining in the line at the Fleet speed and continuing her firing as if she had never been touched. Older ships, as both sides found to their cost, were much more vulnerable. Probably the Turkish ships were the easiest of all to put down, as it is doubtful if their fatalistic officers troubled to keep the water-tight doors closed.

It must be remembered that there is all the difference in the world between a practice and a war attack. The war attack is usually unexpected, and is done under conditions of light and weather which make things chancy, to say the least of it. In a practice attack an officer can afterwards usually plot on the chart for you every movement his boat and the enemy made, and give reasons for all orders he gave. After a war attack he would probably only be able to remember clearly such things as the periscope hoisting gear giving trouble and the hydroplane men appearing to be unaccountably deaf. I have mixed up several boats' attacks in the following description, and it would not be far wrong as an account of more.

2

The mist closed in in swirling clouds that came along the calm water in lines a few hundred yards apart. One moment through the periscope the captain of the L-boat could see across the yellow-green sea a band of fog crossing his bows—the next, he could see nothing but the ripples that spread and vanished astern a few feet from the top prism of the instrument. It had been a poor visibility day since dawn, and now it looked like being thick weather till dark. He called to the first lieutenant and gave an order.

The hydroplane wheels whirred and the boat tilted up and climbed to the accompaniment of sighs and roars, as a couple of external tanks were partly blown. The captain looked down as he climbed the conning-tower ladder: "Slow ahead, port motor—put a charge on starboard—stop blowing." He threw back the lid and met the clammy touch of wet fog on his face. The boat was moving slowly east through a calm sea with only her conning-tower and guns above water, while a white line of foam running forward traced where her deck superstructure ran a few inches below the surface.

If she had been on patrol anywhere but to the west of the

Vyl Lightship the captain would have taken her to seventy feet and kept a hydrophone watch, but that billet is one that marks the end of a German swept channel, and he wanted to watch from above for the first sign of the fog clearing. He sat on the conning-tower lip, his sea-booted legs resting on the third ladder-rung, and his head twisting this way and that as he stared at the white wall of mist that was so close to him.

He had sat there barely a minute, and the booming roar of the big charging engine had just begun sounding up the conning-tower when he slid forward and stood on the ladder with his head and shoulders only exposed; he leaned out to starboard trying to catch again the faint note of a syren that he had felt rather than heard through the note of his own engine.

Then something showed dark through the fog, a grey blur with a line of foam below, and the L-boat's lid clanged down, and through her hull rang the startling, insistent blare of the electric alarm. The engine stopped, the port motor woke to full speed, and the control-room was alive with sound and rapid movement. She inclined down by the bow as the captain's boots appeared down the ladder, and as he jumped to the deck his hasty glance at the gauge showed her to be already at twelve feet. But twelve feet by gauge means a conning-tower top still exposed, and as the tanks filled and the internal noises died down a sound could be heard to starboard—a noise of high-speed engines that swelled till it seemed that every second would bring the crash and roar of water each man could imagine so clearly.

The gauge-needle checked at fifteen, then swung rapidly up to thirty; the faces watching it relaxed slightly—for the noise swelling through the boat told of destroyers, and destroyers are shallow-draught vessels. The boat still raced on down, with the gauge jerking round through 60-70-80. . . ."Hold her up, now—back to seventy, coxswain"; the angle changed swiftly to "bow-up" as the spinning wheels reversed and the boat checked at eighty-five; a pump began to stamp and hammer as it drove out the water from a midship tank, and as the trim settled, the big main motors were steadily eased back to "dead slow." The first lieutenant looked up from the gauge and spoke over his shoulder to the captain. "I made it twelve seconds to twenty feet, sir; what was it that passed?"

"You're a cheery optimist with your twelve seconds. Your watch is stopped, Number One. It's destroyers, and they didn't give us much room either."

"Then d'you mean a fleet? "

"I mean I'm coming up to look in a quarter of an hour. I believe if it wasn't foggy I'd see them on the horizon now; that was a screening force that put us down. Here comes another."

Again the sound of a turbine-driven vessel came from the starboard hand. It swelled to its maximum and then suddenly died to a murmur, passing away to port. Twice more the warning came, and then fell a silence of just five minutes by the captain's wristwatch. "Bring her up—twenty-four feet—and don't break surface now." He turned round to the periscope as the boat climbed and tested the raising gear, making the big shining tube move a few feet up and down.

As the gauge moved to the 30 mark, the periscope rose with a rush, and he bowed his head to the eye-piece in readiness for an early glimpse of the surface world. At twenty-five feet a grunt of satisfaction and a quick swing round of the periscope spoke of his relief at being able to see at all; the fog was clearing and he was diving across one of the long lanes made in the mist by the rising wind. He turned the boat through eight points to keep her in the lane, turning up-wind to meet the clearer visibility that was coming. As he steadied on the new course he stiffened in his crouching attitude, staring to port: "Action Stations—evolution now—get a move on."

The clatter and excitement of flooding tubes and opening doors lasted hardly sixty seconds, but it was punctuated by several sentences from the periscope position such as: "Are you going to get those tubes ready?" and less plaintively, "How much something longer now?" The captain's thoughts were out in the mist above him where his range of view was bounded on two sides by faintly seen grey masses that rushed past him at close range.

The reports of, "Ready, bow tubes"; "beam tubes ready, sir," came through the voice-pipes as the first lieutenant hurried from forward, panting from his exertions.

"All ready, sir," he said, and paused for breath. "What is it, sir; can you see? . . ."

The captain interrupted: "Yes," he said, "blinkin' mist and battle-cruisers. Port beam, stand by; port beam, fire! Starboard twenty-five; stop port, full speed starboard; look out forrard, Number One, I'm going to let go the lot."

The first lieutenant vanished through the control-room door as the familiar sound of a destroyer passing at short range began again to fill the boat. At the periscope the captain swore silently and continuously at the mist, the enemy, and the L-boat. He was between the destroyer screen and the big ships; the whole High Sea Fleet seemed to be coming by, and he had the very vaguest idea of their formation or even of their course. His first torpedo had missed, and it was more than likely the track of it would be seen.

The L-boat spun round under the drive of the screw and the helm she carried, and as two destroyers of the screen converged on her periscope in high fountains of spray, she fired her bow salvo of torpedoes at the nearest of the big dim ships that crossed her bows. The range was short and the salvo ragged, for one torpedo "hung in the tube" a few seconds before leaving, its engines roaring and driving the water from the tube over the men abaft it in a drenching shower.

That torpedo hit the ship astern of and beyond the target— the first bow torpedo to leave exploding right aft on the target herself. The converging destroyers swerved out-wards slightly to avoid mutual collision, and the two "*Wasserbomben*" they dropped as they turned were let go more in anger than with accurate aim. Thirty feet down the L-boat, her forward tanks flooding and her nose down at an angle of 15°, was driving her gauge round in an urgent hurry to gain depth. Seventy—eighty—ninety-five.

"Hold her up now. Blow number two external. Slow both—

dammit, hold her up, man. Stop both—hold on, everybody!"

The gauge-needle went round with a rush; there was a heavy shock, and the boat's bow sprang upwards (the captain, holding with one arm to the periscope and bracing his feet, had a momentary vision in his memory of a photograph of a tank climbing a parapet—a trivial recollection of a Bond Street shop window); she rolled to starboard as the gauge-needle jumped back from a hundred and twenty to the hundred mark, then bounced again as her tail touched, rolled to port, and slid along the bottom to rest on an even keel. Whang-bang-whang.

The explosions of depth-charges passed overhead and made the lights flicker; then a succession of fainter reports continuing to the southward told of a chase misled in the mist. A voice spoke from a tube at the captain's side, "Did they hit, sir?"

The captain was feeling vaguely in his pockets. A reaction from the tense concentration of the last few minutes was approaching, and the habits of an habitual smoker were calling to him. "Yes, I think so," he said; "but there were so many explosions I can't swear to it. We'll know when we get in."

He took a cigarette from his case and lit it. The match burnt blue and went out quickly; the cigarette gave him a mouthful of acrid smoke, and also failed. The short time the conning-tower had been open before the destroyers came had not cleared the air, and the work and excitement of the crew in the attack had consumed as much oxygen as if the boat had been diving for a summer's day. There is only one kind of cigarette which will burn in bad air; a stoker kneeling by the main line flooding-valve fumbled in his cap, and then held out a packet of five of them to the captain. The officer took one with a grunt of thanks, lit it, and spoke again. ' Watch remain at diving-stations—fall out the rest—torpedo hands reload."

3

I am just branching off to the Adriatic a moment to describe a patrol trip by "E 21" (Lieutenant Carlyon Britton). In this account of British submarine doings I have been avoiding such incidents as have been already much better treated of by writers such as Rudyard Kipling and Sir Henry Newbolt. There are, however, a good many incidents for which they had not space in their accounts, and mention of such incidents here will lay stress on the fact that submarine work was continuous throughout the war, and was not a matter of spasmodic effort.

On the 30th June 1918 "E 21," being a unit of our flotilla working with the Italian Navy, torpedoed and sank an Austrian ammunition transport inshore close to Piana, one of the islands that fringe the Dalmatian coast. She then fired at an escorting torpedo-boat (who dodged and saved herself), and she was then bombed by an aeroplane without receiving damage. On the 1st July she charged her batteries in Mid-Adriatic and moved east towards Lissa Island. On arrival there she dived up to St Giorgio harbour (I wonder what Tegetthof would have thought of this sort of thing in 1864?), only turning back a mile from the entrance when it was plain that there were no ships inside. She moved on along the coast and looked into Civita Vecchia, but saw nothing worth attack there.

Between Brazza Island and Lesina Island runs the Greco de Lesina Channel—a gap rather after the pattern of the Dardanelles. "E 21" dived to 130 feet to pass under the minefield which guards the "narrows," and went through by compass and dead reckoning. After four hours she rose and, being then well through the straits, proceeded towards Makarska on the surface. At dawn she dived again and did a sweep round the bay, finding no shipping in the harbours.

Returning that evening, she safely negotiated the minefield at 130 feet depth and proceeded west and north to look at Zero *via* Island, near the locality where she had sunk the transport. She found nothing to fire at there, and the weather getting misty and bad for periscope work, she shaped course back to Brindisi on the 4th. She had been sent out to catch Austrian transports, and having sunk one which was well out on its way, and having been bombed for doing so, she had gone right back along the traffic route to see if "running to heel" would provide another chance, while at the same time her absence would give time for the excitement off Piana to die down. On her return she found it had died down to the extent of nothing being in sight; but her strategy had nevertheless been sound and well conceived.

Aeroplane bombs around the Heligoland Bight became common in 1918. A typical "Aircraft "report comes from "E 56" (Lieutenant Satow) in May of that year. Her station was by the South Dogger Bank Light:—

23rd May.—South Dogger, bearing north 3 miles at 1 a.m. 4.30 a.m.: a Zeppelin in sight N.E.—a long way off. 10 a.m.: sighted seaplane in periscope two miles on port beam coming towards me—dived 60 ft.—altered course to west. 10.15: one bomb—dived to 90 ft.—up to periscope depth and continued patrol. 6.20 p.m.: three bombs—dived to 80 feet. 6.37: three bombs—altered course to N.E., depth 70 feet. 6.50: one bomb. 7.37 p.m.: at 80 feet six or seven bombs dropped, three of them close to boat.

26th May.—Sighted seaplane—dived 70 feet at 4.45 a.m. 9 a.m.: sighted seaplane—dived 80 feet. 9.38: five bombs dropped. 12.15: one bomb dropped. Heard propellers which passed on. 4 p.m.: two bombs dropped. 4.20: one bomb dropped. Heard propellers and sweep. 4.40 p.m.: two bombs—propellers and sweep. 6.20 p.m.: one bomb a long way off—propellers heard—boat rolled in the wash of destroyers.

28th May.—4.45 a.m.: Sighted seaplanes bearing east. 3.20 p.m.: sighted Zeppelin bearing north.

All bombs mentioned in this report were small ones.

The attentions paid to "E 56" on the 26th call to mind the story of the E-boat which did a "crash dive" to avoid similar machines. The captain arrived at the foot of the conning-tower with a rush, his binoculars preceding him with a heavy thud and his oilskin coming after him; as he touched the deck three bombs exploded on the surface just over his boat, the shock making him sit down suddenly.

To the first lieutenant's unspoken question of "What is it after us?" he answered with an absurd giggle, and "They've evidently seen me!" Students of Captain Bairnsfather's drawings will catch the allusion.

4

I will conclude the accounts of typical submarine *v.* submarine engagements by the case of "E 34" (Lieutenant Pulleyne) and a U-boat off Harwich on the 10th May 1918.

"E 34" was returning to harbour after a trip. She was actually in the swept channel leading into Harwich, and could pretty well take it for granted that any vessel met with so near home would be friendly. As boats get near their base it is usual to begin the cleaning-up work which is so necessary after a trip, and to get ready generally for harbour routine again. "E 34" saw a submarine ahead steering north, and, treating her as hostile until her identity could be established, dived at once to attack. Fifteen minutes later Lieutenant Pulleyne, in no doubt at all about what his target's nationality was, fired both bow tubes and sank her. He then rose, and proceeded to pick up the only survivor, who happened to be the captain, and who was in pretty bad condition from shock and immersion.

Captain (S.), H.M.S. *Maidstone*, comments on the affair as follows:—

> I am pleased to be able to record that, with the two submarines meeting end on—the one in enemy waters and the other just returning to base after a somewhat difficult mine-laying operation—it was the submarine which might have been expected to have been least on the *qui vive* which scored the success. This reflects great credit on Lieutenant Pulleyne and his ship's company, as it shows they were in all respects ready.

It is probable that this incident caused a number of our other officers secretly to wonder whether, in "E 34's" place, they would have been equally successful and prompt.

The captain of the U-boat was a charming prisoner. He was taken aboard the *Maidstone* and put in a cabin under medical care. His clothes were dried and other clothes given him. When he had recovered he went off to a prisoners' camp, from whence he wrote peremptory letters to the *Maidstone* officers accusing them of having stolen his waistcoat, and presenting a bill for its value if not instantly returned.

The *Maidstone* view of the matter was that they hadn't got his beastly waistcoat, didn't believe he'd ever had one, and wouldn't touch it with a barge-pole if he had. Considering they could not have treated him with more consideration if he had been one of themselves, and that incidentally they had saved his life—well, the Hun is a queer person and we'll never be able to understand him.

The story of the sinking of "E 14" (Lieutenant-Commander White) in the Dardanelles has already appeared in print, so I shall not tell it again. But the thought of German submarine officers leads to comparisons, and perhaps a submarine sailor had better give his views about it here:—

Copy of letter received by H.M.S. *Adamant* from Petty Officer R. A. Perkins (late of S/M "E 14"), Prisoner of War, No. 5456, Fabrique de Cement, Eski Hissar, Guebzeh, Asia Minor.

Dear Sir,—No doubt the officers and men of the *Adamant* and submarines would like to know what became of the captain and two officers. I am very sorry to say that Mr White was almost blown to pieces by a large shell which wounded three other men, and I believe it killed Mr Drew, as I was with both of them. I saw the captain's body, but nothing of Mr Drew, so I think he must have been killed and fell into the sea. Mr Blasset was last seen in the engine-room, so went down with the boat.

It was a credit to us all to think that we had such a brave captain, and, sir, if only I could mention a few things about him; but owing to his coolness he saved the boat half a dozen times. It is a great pity that no officer was saved to tell the tale. I also mention A.B. Mitchell and Signalman Trimbell for gallantry in diving overboard and saving the life of Prichard, Ord. Tel., who was badly wounded, and would have lost his life had it not been for both of these men keeping him afloat until assistance arrived.

I am glad to say that all men that were wounded were sent to hospital ten minutes after being captured, and were treated very well. The remaining five men, except Stoker Reed, have had a bad attack of fever since being captured. We are all sorry that so few men were saved, and, as I have said, our gallant captain. This is all I have to report.

Being the senior survivor, Petty Officer Perkins reports as such. If his officers had lived I think it probable we would have heard something to the credit of Petty Officer Perkins.

The escape of Lieutenant-Commander Cochrane from Asia Minor is being described in *Maga*. The account of how he became a prisoner seems to indicate that he was not likely to remain a submissive captive:—

6.30 a.m.: Passed Kilid Bahr at 200 yards— the periscope being fired on by the forts without result.

7.30: Sighted the buoys of the submarine net off Nagara Point. Dived to 100 feet and increased to 7½ knots.
The bows cut through the net as the starboard propeller fouled and stopped the starboard motor. Went hard-a-port and port motor to full speed. Boat fell off to port and lay parallel to and much entangled in the net. I tried to turn the boat's head to south and pass through the net.

8.30 a.m.: A mine exploded a few hundred feet from the boat, no damage being done.
After about two hours manoeuvring the boat was turned to the southward, and repeated attempts to get clear were made at depths of from 60 to 130 feet by going full speed ahead and astern. Boat was now held by the net fore and aft.

10.30 a.m.: A mine was exploded close to the boat. The explosion was violent, but no damage was done to the hull. After this explosion the boat was much freer than before, *and in the hopes that further attempts to blow up the boat might result in completely freeing her,*[1] I decided to remain submerged at a good depth till after dark, when it might be possible to come to the surface and clear the obstruction. Burned all confidential papers.

By 2 p.m. battery power was much reduced and further attempts to get clear were given up for a time.

6.40 p.m.: A mine was exploded a few feet from the hull; the explosion was very violent—electric lights and other small fittings being broken. The motors were at once started in the hope that the net had been destroyed; but this was not the case. The presence of enemy craft on the surface having made it impossible to come to the surface after dark and so clear the obstruction, I decided to come up and remove the crew from the boat before blowing her up.

The boat was brought to the surface without difficulty, and when the conning-tower was above water Lieutenant Scaife went on deck to surrender the crew. Fire was immediately opened on him from light guns on shore and three motor-boats which were lying round 'E 7.' As soon as the excitement had died down and the enemy officers had regained control of their men, two motor-boats came alongside and the officers and men were taken off without difficulty. This operation was carried out under the orders of German submarine officers. The boat was sunk as soon as she was clear of men, and a time-fuse having been fired, subsequently blew up.

Throughout the day the discipline and behaviour of the crew was excellent. This was particularly noticeable at the time of the third explosion. At this time the crew had

---

1 The italics are mine.—Author.

been fallen out from their stations, and many of them were asleep. On being called to their stations every man went quietly to his place, although the violence of the explosion was such as to convince everyone that the boat was badly damaged.

... Petty Officer Sims, L.T.O., was in charge of the after-switchboard, and continued throughout the day to work the starboard motor, although much hampered by smoke and pieces of molten copper, due to the damage received by the motor and starting resistances while freeing the propeller.

Lieutenant-Commander Cochrane attempted to escape, but after covering 200 miles was, with Lieutenant-Commander Stoker of "AE 2," captured ten miles from the coast. They received a year's imprisonment, and on August 18, 1918, Lieutenant-Commander Cochrane started his successful trip, accompanied by seven military officers, back to England.

CHAPTER 5

Evolution & Action

In 1916 we began to look to Germany to produce something very unpleasant in the way of submarines. We were certain she would follow the obvious course indicated by the lessons all belligerents were learning, and produce the big U-cruiser. Very fortunately for us, she produced nothing of the sort until well into 1918, when one small U-cruiser did us a great deal of damage. The point was this—We were worrying and chasing U-boats with trawlers, motor-boats, destroyers, and numbers of other comparatively small and weakly-armed craft.

If a U-cruiser, armed with, say, four 6-inch guns, and armoured along her top-strakes, had risen to fight her tormentors—well, it is clear that our small patrol-vessel service would have become suddenly very expensive. Each convoy would have required cruiser protection, and we had not enough cruisers to provide this.

In 1917, by our constructor's reckonings, there was no reason why a German submarine could not have been produced which could proceed safely to the East Indies (round the Cape), and repeat (on a bigger scale) the exploits of the *Emden*. Well, the Germans didn't do it; they produced U-cruisers with two 5.9" guns apiece in 1918, but the type was unsatisfactory and unstable.

It is still a puzzle to us that the idea came to them so slowly. We had K-class boats with the fleet in 1916 of 2600 tons, and had shown that a big submarine was a working proposition. (The K boat, of course, is not a cruiser-submarine; she is a fast and lightly-gunned type for use in battle only, and she does not leave the fleet except when detached for watching patrols.) We produced the M-class in 1917, and—for obvious reasons—we kept the type as secret as possible until the Armistice.

The M boat is rather smaller than the K, and is of only seventeen knots speed, but she has far better under-water capabilities than her big companion. She carries, besides her torpedo armament, a 12-inch gun of the normal battleship type. This gun can be carried loaded submerged by the use of a watertight tampion and breech. The boat can rise in the wake of an enemy, fire as she "breaks surface," and submerge again—all in a matter of seconds.

The type was extremely successful, and one can only be thankful that such boats were not on the enemy's side. They would have been the very devil to deal with on the trade routes, and would have caused us to reconsider very hurriedly our whole system of anti-submarine defence. Of course, four 6-inch would be better than one 12-inch from a German point of view, especially as a destroyer would be likely to attack unscathed under the fire of one big gun, but our type was intended for use against such things as enemy cruisers, and not for sinking merchant ships.

By the end of the war the enemy had arrived at the stage of submarine design where one says, "We've got a type that works—let us stick to it, and just add improvements." We passed that stage before the war and are now in the confident (with reservations) state of feeling that we can turn out anything required to combine the properties of under-water and surface craft. If submarines continue as weapons of war, they will improve very considerably, and the range of possibility of future types is so great that any prophecy now would be rash. It must be remembered, however, that the depth of water in which a boat is intended to operate limits her size.

It is not only that the distance from her keel to periscope is (in the case of a big boat) some 50 feet, but also that the great length of a big boat's hull means that even a slight fore-and-aft inclination as she dives will add enormously to her draught; a very long boat in twenty fathoms of water (the North Sea average) would have to be careful not to get off an even keel, as it might happen that in the presence of the enemy her bow or stern would touch bottom, with the result of causing the whole boat to bounce up to the surface.

A submarine submerged is in a state of equilibrium, in that she has little or no tendency to rise or sink if her motors are stopped and the boat left to herself. I am afraid in this history that I continue to speak of submarines as if everybody knew a good deal about them. I use technical expressions and words as if I was dealing with things like motor-cars. I will try and explain more clearly what I mean by "bouncing to the surface," and will do so in the idea that there are probably readers who know as much about diving boats as I do of bimetallism.

A submarine is a surface ship which can be submerged and driven ahead at a steady depth-line. She is built strongly in order to resist the water-pressure when she is deep down. She is propelled on the surface by (usually) heavy-oil Diesel engines. When submerged she cannot use these, as they consume air, so she has an electric battery and motors for use under water. The battery is charged when on the surface at her convenience or by favour of the enemy. The Diesel engines are used for this purpose, and they recharge the batteries through the motors, using the latter as dynamos.

In old pictures of projected submarines of the seventeenth century one sees that the principle of "trimming down" for submersion was known, and that our present-day system of tanks was intended to be substituted by pig-skins which fitted into cylindrical hollows in the hull. These skins were emptied by screwing out a ram from inside (on the idea of old-fashioned printing presses) which squashed the skins.

Nowadays a boat is all tanks along her lower half, the upper half being living space and battery room, etc. These tanks are flooded through valves in order to destroy the boat's buoyancy. The water is ejected from them either by pumps or by the use of compressed air, the latter taking the place of the old seven-teenth-century screw-press idea. When the tanks have flooded until the boat's buoyancy is all gone—*i.e.,* until you could press her down or lift her up with one hand—she is "trimmed," and by going ahead and working the bow and stern hydroplanes you can keep whatever depth-line is required.

When submerged, a lookout is kept through a periscope—a tube about thirty feet long which has lenses all the way up, is watertight, and has an eyepiece like an ordinary telescope at its lower end.

To dive, a boat opens her vents, puts "dive" helm on, and goes under with her motors running. The flooding valves are kept open to save time; in surface trim a boat is "hanging on the vents"—*i.e.,* if you open the vents (upper valves of the tanks) the water enters and she goes down; until the vents are open the wa-ter cannot enter beyond a certain point; when they do open the air in the tanks can get away and the tanks fill up with a rush.

During a trip the "trim" of the boat alters continually. She is using fuel, ammunition, food, and water, and calculation is necessary to allow for this. Certain tanks are used for this com-pensating, so that on all occasions when a rapid dive is necessary, there is nothing to do but flood the big external tanks, and yet know that the boat will be in hand when under. If mistakes are made, they will show at once.

If too much has been put into the "internals" to compensate, the boat will run on down to the bottom in spite of "up helm" and full speed. If too little, you have to flood internals accord-ing to an estimate of what is needed as she ploughs along half-sub-merged; the latter case is one to be avoided, as you may be killed by the enemy while flooding. The usual war practice is to compensate on the "heavy" side—*i.e.,* let her go with a rush and blow tanks so as to catch her and hold her at sixty feet; then you can bring her up to patrol depth at your leisure.

It can be seen, then, that the description of a boat as "bounc-ing" is not incorrect. When going to the bottom for the night it is a common occurrence, if too rough a "landing" is made, to proceed like a tennis-ball along the sand for a couple of hundred yards. It is a curious thing that both in the Cattegat and the Sea of Marmora, boats have been able to lie for the night with motors stopped at depths of from thirty to seventy feet. In the Marmora the junction depth of the salt and fresh water is about seventy.

A boat trimmed with about two hundred pounds of negative buoyancy out there will, if she stops her motors, sink slowly through the upper layer of fresh (or brackish) water, till she meets the denser salt below; on reaching this she will be in a state of "positive" buoyancy, and after a little bouncing up and down to find her "zero" *stratum*, she will settle at a steady depth. The same sort of thing—a blessing in the Marmora—is a nuisance in the Bight. A boat crossing the mouths of the German rivers may be at one moment diving comfortably with zero helm on the hydroplanes—the next, she meets a layer of fresh water from the Jahde ebb and is bumping on the bottom with "hard-up" helm and the pumps working on the tanks.

2

The exploits of "E 11" in the Dardanelles have been published during the war; this boat, however, did not begin her war career in the Sea of Marmora—she had already shown her usual attitude of contemptuous familiarity towards the enemy when on patrol in the Heligoland Bight. On one occasion in 1914 she certainly met a "ghost"—*i.e.*, something which never gave any satisfactory explanation of what it was. "E 11" was diving in sight of Heligoland, and having sighted a line of four destroyers coming over her horizon, she turned in to attack them.

Suddenly her bow was jerked up to a startling angle, and tanks had to be hastily flooded to prevent a "break surface." The boat then seemed to go crazy—taking angles by the bow or stern apparently in defiance of all laws of hydrostatics. The captain made up her mind for her by running her down to the bottom in 65 feet and holding her there. In a few minutes the sound of screws came from overhead, and the same sound continued for several minutes. "E 11" was then dived up off the bottom, but was found to be still in the same strange condition, taking up this time an angle of 20 degrees up by the bow. She was once more taken down and held to the bottom, while again screws passed by and curious noises came from overhead.

The noises went on for an hour, during which time the officers and crew—with the business-like decision of the British nation—had tea. When the noises had stopped "E 11" was again lifted, when she showed a perfect trim and instant obedience to her hydroplanes, proceeding along at her normal patrol depth as if she had never given any trouble at all. Nothing was in sight through the periscope except Heligoland, and the explanation of "E 11's" hysteria is still her own secret.

The same boat, as was reported at the time, shared a Christmas dinner with some representatives of the R.N.A.S. on the day of the 1914 Cuxhaven air raid. The Germans have not given us their version of what happened, but from the following it will be seen that it is a pity that they did not publish an uncensored story.

At 11 a.m. "E 11" was diving on her billet to the westward of Norderney, when she saw through the periscope a seaplane coming out to seaward and flying low. She came to the surface, and, having been placed on that billet "according to plan," was not surprised to find that the machine was British. The seaplane took the water safely, and "E 11" took her in tow with the idea of saving the machine. The pilot (carrying his confidential bomb-sight with him) was taken on board first.

Hardly had the tow started when two more seaplanes were seen approaching from the direction of the shore, one of them flying very groggily and looking like an imitation of a tumbler pigeon. "E 11" stopped and the machines closed her; so did a large Schutte-Lanz type airship, which was presumably in pursuit of them. Of the two seaplanes the undamaged one came down comfortably close to the submarine, and then all spectators stood up to watch the alighting of the other, which was seen to have had its tail shot off and to be under the nominal control of its ailerons only. Everybody held their breath as the pilot brought the machine down, and there was a general groan of sympathy as the crash came. She pitched nose first into the sea, and it looked as though the pilot could hardly have survived; then a wet figure was seen to climb slowly out of the wreck and perch cross-legged on the tip of the broken tail.

By this time the enemy airship had arrived, and "E 11" realised that speed in picking up the seaplane pilots was becoming more advisable every minute. An additional complication chose this moment to turn up in the shape of a U-boat, [1] which appeared on the surface about two miles away and then dived—presumably to attack with torpedoes. "E 11" at this stage of the war was unfortunately not fitted with a gun. She slipped tow from Number One seaplane and fired several revolver bullets through its floats to ensure its sinking.

She then closed Number Two and took the pilot and observer off her just as the airship arrived overhead at a height of two hundred feet. The faces of the Germans in the gondolas could be clearly seen, and the men in the middle car were displaying considerable activity—probably wrestling with a faulty bomb-dropping gear. Before the bombing business was in working order, however, the light breeze had carried the airship down to leeward—much to the relief of "E 11," who saw the enemy restart her engines in order to make a sweep round and get into position again. "E 11" having punctured the floats of Number Two seaplane with bullets, manoeuvred alongside Number Three, and picked up a very wet pilot and mechanic.

By this time there was every probability of the U-boat having approached inside easy torpedo range—in fact "E 11" was wondering why the expected torpedoes were so slow in arriving. For this reason, and also because the airship was now nearly back overhead again, any further delay was rash, and so the pilot and mechanic were unceremoniously hustled below, and "E 11" demonstrated to them what a "crash-dive" was like from inside. The depth gauges had just reached nineteen feet when

1 Later discovered to be another E-boat.

two heavy explosions occurred on the surface,—the enemy's bomb-dropping gear was working nicely again, but too late. "E 11" went under feeling a little hurt at having had to leave a job unfinished; she had meant to sink Number Three seaplane before leaving, and was unhappy at the idea of it being still of use to the enemy.

On rising sufficiently to use her periscope, however, she was delighted to observe the Schutte-Lanz venting its hate in machine-gun fire on the abandoned machine—an expenditure of ammunition which continued until the sorely-tried raider sank. "E 11" was for a moment inclined to come up to pass a polite signal of thanks to the enemy, but, after consultation, it was decided that humour was wasted on Germans, and so the boat was taken on to the bottom for a rest while the Xmas dinner was disposed of. The five passengers shared the dinner, and presumably enjoyed the day, but it blew half a gale and more all the way home to Harwich, and the motion of an "E" boat takes a lot of getting used to.

Everybody has read of the doings of this submarine in the Sea of Marmora, and I will try to avoid writing about despatches already published; but I think the actions between submarines and soldiers have been perhaps only lightly touched on, in view of the fact that such actions are so unique in their nature and circumstances.

In August 1915 "E 14" and "E 11" met at a rendezvous in the Marmora with the intention of acting on "information received." "E 11" says:—

August 7th, 5 a.m.: Dived by Dohan Aslan Buoy, keeping watch on road.

11.30 a.m.: Observed troops on road leading towards Gallipoli. Rose to surface and opened fire, several shots dropping well amongst them, causing them to scatter. Observed column approaching along same road. Range of the road now being known from our position, dropped several shells among them. Column took cover in open order.

1.10 p.m.: Large column observed on road nearer Gallipoli, marching at high speed. Opened fire, but failed to stop progress of column, although a large number of dead and wounded appeared to be left alongside the road. This column was under fire for about half an hour, when we were forced to dive by shore guns.

3.20 p.m.: Hose to surface and opened fire at a considerable body of troops, apparently resting. They immediately dispersed, and subsequently opened a well-directed fire with a field gun. Dived."

"E 14" (her captain, Commander Boyle, was senior to Commander Nasmith of "E 11") says :—

August 7th . . . at 1.30 p.m.: I saw more dust coming down the road. Rose to the surface, and opened fire on troops marching towards Gallipoli. "E 11" was firing at the time I came up. I had stationed her to the north-east of Dohan Aslan Bank, and she first shelled the troops on a part of the road showing there, and then came down to my billet, where we both shelled them for the best part of an hour. I got off forty rounds, and about six of them burst in the middle of the troops. I had to put full range on the sights and aim at the top of the hill, so my shooting was not very accurate. "E 11" having a 12-pdr., did much more damage, and scattered the troops several times. Soon after 2 p.m. they started firing on us from the shore and out-ranging us."

"E 11" on August 18th :—

7 a.m.: Rose to surface near Dohan Aslan Buoy to bombard troops, but they scattered before fire was opened.

8.30 a.m.: Rose to surface and opened fire on large convoy on road, several shells falling among them before they managed to scatter.

9 a.m.: Observed fire springing up where our shots had fallen. This rapidly increased in size, until in the afternoon

and evening it had assumed very large proportions.

A U-boat was captured by cavalry in 1918, but that case was perhaps exceptional. In the Napoleonic wars it was customary for English frigates to fire at French troops marching along the coast-roads of Spain, so that the E boats in the Marmora were only repeating history, but they certainly showed that the new weapon was a most disconcerting one for troops to have to reply to.

I do not intend to fill pages with unexplained despatches, but the following extracts explain themselves, and, in any case, are too good to be omitted from any submarine history.

"E 11" (Commander Nasmith) :—

May 23rd, 5.50 a.m.: Observed Turkish torpedo-gunboat at anchor off Constantinople. Attacked and sank her with port-bow torpedo, striking her amidships on the starboard side. While sinking she opened fire with a 6-pdr. gun, the first round hitting the foremost periscope. Proceeded to position north of Kalolimno Island. Rose to surface, and prepared damaged periscope for new top.

10.30 a.m.: Hands to bathe.

May 24th, 10.30 a.m.: Observed small steamer proceeding to the westward. Examined vessel through periscope, and rose to surface on her port quarter. Signalled her to stop. No notice was taken. Brought her to a standstill by several rounds from a rifle directed at her bridge. Ordered crew to abandon the ship. This they carried out with reckless haste, capsizing all but one boat.

Fortunately with this boat they were able to right the other two and pick up those swimming in the water. An American gentleman then appeared on the upper deck, who informed us that his name was Silas Q. Swing, of the *Chicago Sun*, and that he was pleased to make our ac-quaintance. He then informed us that the steamer was proceeding to Chanak with Turkish marines, and that he was not sure if there were any stores on board.

Ran up alongside and put Lieutenant D'Oyly-Hughes on board with demolition party. He discovered a 6-inch gun lashed across the top of the fore-hatch—the forehold containing one large 6-inch gun mounting and several small 12-pdr. pedestals, the guns for which were probably at the bottom of the hold.

The after-hold was full of 6-inch projectiles, and on top of this were resting about fifty large white-metal cartridge-cases marked Krupp. The demolition charge was then placed against the ship's side in the after-hold, well tamped with 6-inch shells and cartridges. All hands returned to the boat and the charge was fired. The vessel exploded with a loud report, and a large column of smoke and flame shot up.

At 11.15 a.m. "E 11" dived into Rodosto harbour after a heavily-laden store-ship. At 12.35 she torpedoed her as she lay along-side the pier. In the afternoon she missed a paddle-steamer which managed to save herself by beaching.

On the 25th "E 11" dived into Constantinople and torpedoed a steamer along-side the arsenal. On the 28th she sank a large supply ship. On the 31st she torpedoed a large vessel lying in Panderma Roads. On June 2nd she got another, which was probably—from the violence of the explosion—laden with ammunition. On June 7th, on her way out of the Sea of Marmora, "E 11" sank a large troopship and so finished her cruise. I am quoting these statistics to point out what damage may be done by a single submarine on an army's line of communication.

The moral effect (in such ways as delaying and scaring traffic) is, of course, as great as the material, and probably far greater.

The Marmora submarines hardly deign to mention such small fry as *dhows* and other sailing ships, but the list runs to a great length when put together. Here are a few days' sinkings by "E 14" (Commander Boyle). On June 20th she sank three *dhows*, on the 22nd one, on the 23rd a two-masted sailing-ship, on the 24th two *dhows*, and on the 27th a brigantine.

Nowadays a submarine on that sort of duty would have to

expect all kinds of retaliation and unpleasantness, but at that stage of the war the anti-submarine work was feeble, and the enemy must have cursed at his own impotence to defend his sea routes.

"E 12" (Commander Bruce) was the boat that had the battle at ten yards' range with an armed tug in the Sea of Marmora. She came victorious out of the action, having sunk her opponent. She had a habit of using her one gun in a violent manner which caused much distress to the enemy. On the 16th September 1916, on a trip up the Dardanelles, she torpedoed a munition steamer in Burgas Bay. On the 18th, being then inside the Marmora, she

> Dived into Rodosto, but found nothing. Chased torpedo-boat of the 'Antalia' class off Kalolimno Island. We both opened fire at about 8000 yards, the torpedo-boat turning towards us. The fourth shot hit her aft, and she then turned and proceeded at high speed towards Constantinople, seeming to be on fire aft.

The Turkish anti-submarine craft must have been in the position of the darkey who hooked the alligator—*Is dis nigger fishing, or is dis fish a-niggerin'*?

"E 12" continues unmoved—

> Proceeded into Mudania, bombarded Magazine outside town, hit it eight times, silenced the batteries which opened fire on us and damaged the railway. Sank two sail and proceeded towards Gulf of Ismid.

Nothing was seen in Ismid owing to fog, and so she tried the vicinity of Marmora Island, where on the 21st she sank a steamer of 3000 tons and six *dhows*. Things were dull till the 28th, when she sank three off Ismid. On the 29th she met with anti-submarine work again.

> Sank one sail off Rodosto. Destroyer came out, but returned again on sighting us, . . . we were opened fire on from Sar Kioi. Opened fire on them and silenced their

guns. Sank four sail three miles farther to the westward. Aeroplane dropped two bombs, the nearest falling 30 yards from our stern.

On the 5th October she sank a small steamer and seventeen sail in Rodosto Bay. An aeroplane dropped a bomb at her with no success. On the 9th she chased a torpedo-boat on the surface, but was unable to get within range. On the 12th she sank another steamer, and on the 17th submarine "H 1" having come up the Dardanelles also, the two boats chased a gunboat and, getting each side of her, gave her an unhappy time. They hit her several times and she appeared to have lost control, as she nearly went ashore on Kalolimno Point. Eventually she found shelter in Panderma. "E 12" dived in after her, but owing to fog could not see her. Both boats waited patiently all night in hopes of her coming out, but were disappointed. On the 19th "E 12" fired on Constantinople powder factory and had hit it three times before 5·9 in. guns opened fire on her from the shore and made her dive.

On the 25th "E 12" returned down the Narrows. Her experience with the net should be read, remembering that she was an old boat and not meant to stand deep-water pressures.

She passed through the net at 80 feet depth and carried a portion of it with her. This portion must have had some of the heavy weights attached that had been holding the net down, for as the boat came through she took a big angle down by the bow and sank.

The forward hydroplanes caught in the net jammed at "10° of dive." "E 12's" external tanks were blown out and full speed put on the motors. The boat continued down, however, and as the pressure increased, the conning-tower glass scuttles burst in and the conning-tower filled up, the hull leaked forward, and the fore compartment had to be closed off. By putting three men on the wheel the bow hydroplanes were moved a little, and after ten minutes at 245 feet the boat started to rise.

They managed to check her at 12 feet, but found her almost uncontrollable. Six patrol boats opened fire as the conning-tower showed above water, and then the panting hydro-plane men forced her down again. The boat continued to dive badly (she was still towing the net and sinkers), and twice she ran down to 120 feet. Both diving gauges had failed and the gyroscopic compass had followed suit. The conning-tower (magnetic) compass was flooded out and useless.

Then at 80 feet she struck chain moorings off Kelid Bahr and scraped past. This broke away the length of net she had been towing, and released of the weight she rose at once, and before the tanks could be filled again broke surface. The shore batteries and patrol vessels opened lire at once, hitting the conning-tower full with a small shell and sending other small shells and splinters through the bridge. As the boat went down (the conning-tower being flooded already, the shell hole was nothing to worry about) a torpedo fired from Kelid Bahr passed over her, and another 50 yards astern of her. "E 12" continued her dive towards home, her trim and control being then normal. She observed two large explosions a couple of miles astern of her and saw the track of another torpedo, but was not further molested, and joined the Dardanelles Fleet a few hours later.

Submarine "H 1" (Lieutenant Pirie) has been mentioned as having worked in company with "E 12." An "H" boat is, of course, much smaller and less seaworthy than an "E," being of 400 tons and 150 feet length. Before meeting "E 12" at the rendezvous, this boat had sunk a steamer. Later she sank three more steamers and a *dhow*. As "E 12" was leaving the Marmora first, she politely took "H l's" mails out with her.

"E 7" (Commander Cochrane) made herself unpopular with the enemy in July of 1915. She passed up the Dardanelles (being missed "overhead "by a torpedo fired from Kelid Bahr) on the 30th June, and on 2nd July sank a steamer and two *dhows* in Rodosto Bay. On the 3rd she sank a brigantine, and on the 6th a 200-ton Zebec and another brigantine. On the 7th she got a tug and a ferry-steamer and had an action on the surface with a two-or three-gun gunboat which retired, leaving a *dhow* to its fate. In the evening she chased a ferry-steamer ashore. In the morning she sighted the same ferry-steamer under way and sank her.

On the 9th she got a Zebec, and on the 10th she dived into Mudania and torpedoed a steamer alongside the pier. On the 11th she sank two *dhows*, and on the 15th she dived into Constantinople and fired a torpedo at the Arsenal (which is close to the water) in the hope of detonating something. The explosion was very heavy when the torpedo hit. She then dived out and came to the surface off Zeitunlik Powder Mills, into which she fired twelve rounds.

On the 16th she sank a *dhow*, and at 9.30 a.m. on the 17th she opened fire on a railway cutting a mile west of Kaya Burnu and blocked the line. She then waited till she saw a heavy troop train going west, and chased at full speed to pick up the fruits of her labours. The train entered the cutting, and, as was expected, backed out again into Yarandje Station. "E 7" settled down to work, and after twenty rounds had been fired, three ammunition cars blew up. Later in the day she shelled another train and hit several cars, without, however, doing so much damage. She concluded an interesting day by sinking another *dhow*.

On the 18th she sank a brigantine, and was fired at by rifles from Mudania. She replied by hitting a steamer with one shell, and the buildings from which rifles were being fired with ten. Three shells fired into a small shed on the beach produced heavy and satisfactory explosions.

On the 19th she sank four sail, and on the 21st one; on the 22nd she fired again on a train rounding Kaya Burnu and on a stone railway bridge. On the 24th she came back through the Narrows, presumably to the immense relief of the Turks. On her next trip, as has already been related, "E 7" was sunk and the crew captured. The coxswain was imprisoned some 60 miles from the coast of Asia Minor. He made a small canvas boat, carried it with him to the beach across that 60 miles of hills and put to sea. He was blown back by a gale, however, and recaptured on the day that his captain escaped from a camp 300 miles inland.

In these interminable lists of sinkings of unarmed vessels it may appear to the reader as if the work had been done roughly and without consideration for the lives of non-combatants. The following report from the commanding officer of the flotilla should be noted:—

> The destruction of the enemy's means of transport in the Sea of Marmora has been pursued throughout with the utmost regard for humanity. Ships carrying refugees have invariably been spared, and the crews of sailing vessels either given time to escape or rescued at considerable inconvenience to the submarine. On many occasions the craws of vessels destroyed have shown their surprise and gratitude at the consideration shown to them.

The first boat to enter the Narrows was "B 11" (Lieutenant Holbrook). She successfully torpedoed and sank the Turkish battleship *Messudiyeh*. The outstanding fact of this feat was that the boat was built in the summer of 1906, making her well over eight years old when she went into the Dardanelles. Eight years is a great age for a submarine in a Service which advances every month in the knowledge of construction, and "B 11" was in 1914 almost ready for a final paying off. She showed, however, that the old boats were by no means useless if handled as they should be.

The first trip right into the Marmora was by "A-E 2" (Lieutenant-Commander Stoker). She was an Australian boat of the same type as the other E's. She was unfortunately sunk by a destroyer in the Marmora after getting in. [2]

In the Baltic also, at the beginning of the war, targets were far more plentiful than in the North Sea. Commander Horton in "E 9" sank a destroyer on January 29, 1915. On June 4 he sank a transport which was protected by a destroyer screen. On July 2 he torpedoed and badly damaged the *Prinz Adalbert*. On July 29 "E 1" (Commander Laurence) sank a transport. On August 19 he torpedoed and damaged the *Moltke*, incidentally causing

---

2. As I have not the despatch by me, I am postponing the account of her passage till later.

the enemy to withdraw from the attack on the Gulf of Riga—
an attack which at the moment showed every probability of
succeeding. Later in the war the Germans renewed their attack
successfully—secure in the knowledge that the internal conditions caused by the Revolution had prevented the British submarines from operating.

At that time we had in the Baltic four "E" Class ("E 18,"
Lieutenant -Commander Halahan, having been lost at sea in
May 1916 with all hands, from a cause unknown) and four "C"
Class. The latter boats had, instead of entering the Baltic by the
Sound, come in August 1916 *via* the White Sea and up the Dvi-
na river in wooden barges towed by tugs; they came practically
empty, and their batteries, etc., were replaced in them on arrival
at Petrograd. The Revolution caused such chaos that the flotilla
was practically tied to harbour after the Soviet Government's
installation.

"C 27" (Lieutenant Sealy), however, was able to torpedo a
transport during the attack on Oesel, and was also reported to
have damaged one of the screening vessels. There is no doubt
that the knowledge that these submarines had been rendered
powerless enormously helped the Germans in the Baltic. Perhaps the best tribute to their efficiency is the insertion by the
enemy in the Peace Treaty with Russia of a clause insisting on
the British boats' destruction. On April 5, 1918, the boats were
blown up and the crews came home overland.

Curious stories were brought back by the returning officers
and men of Revolutionary conditions. The English were not
molested, but were still apparently respected by the Russian sailors. One unfortunate seaman of the Revolutionary Navy had
insulted one of our officers, who complained to the Council
about it. The wretched man was arrested, and would have been
executed if the officer had not personally begged for his life.
This being granted, the man was brought across to the E boat
to apologise.

His mates assisted him to do this by rubbing his face on the
iron deck before the lieutenant-commander's feet. He was then

sent indefinitely to Siberia. The same men who took such steps to uphold politeness to England and her officers at that date, had already brutally hacked numbers of their own officers to pieces, and had drenched their Admiral in paraffin and set a light to him.

When the inevitable end came, and the German transports were approaching, an effort was made to get both British and Russian submarines to sea. The following incident is hardly credible, but I believe it is true: one Russian boat on leaving harbour did a dive for practice—a very wise thing to do.

Her after-hatch was open, and should have been closed on the order to dive. It was not closed, for the simple reason that the man whose duty it was to close it was having his "Stand easy" at the time, and therefore considered the order to shut down to be unconstitutional. He was near the hatch himself, and he sat there and watched the Baltic come in as the boat went under; if ever anybody died for his principles that man did. However, the captain and first lieutenant of the boat escaped as she sank, and were court-martialled for losing their ship. By a nightmare of Revolutionary logic they were sent to Siberia, the court finding that the order to shut down was illegal and harsh, in that certain of the crew were taking their rest, and could not be expected to obey any order.

The E boats at that time had a number of Russian officers on board who had come to them for protection. It was customary for the Russian crews to vote for their captains, and as the life of a captain (controlled by a Council of the crew) was a short and precarious one, it was not uncommon for a new leader of a poll to desert by swimming to the British flotilla. When the flotilla was eventually destroyed by its own officers, Captain Cromie remained to make a last effort to bring the fighting forces back to the Allies' side. As is known to all the world, he closed with his death on the Embassy stairs a chapter of history that our Navy will never have cause to be ashamed of.

Revolutionary crews in Russian submarines gave illustrations of what happens if democracy is carried to its limits. An English submarine officer did a short trip in a boat belonging to the Russian Navy, and his comment about it was that "if it had not been so serious it would have been comic." The crew's committee had dismissed the engineer and mechanicians for reasons of their own, with the result that furious altercations used to go on as to the best way to start up the engines. The results were not always successful; but the cook, who seemed to be the only man aboard who knew how it was done, used to eventually intervene and make the much-enduring metal get to work again. This, of course, was at sea and near to the enemy.

Some difficulties were experienced in keeping the British submarine sailors away from the Russians when the boats were in harbour. Captain Cromie reported on one occasion: "I regret to report that striking cases are becoming more frequent, chiefly due to insolence on the part of the Russians and a growing contempt for them on the part of our men."

Our sailors had no objection to anybody's political opinions, but they did object to a spirit of murder in substitution for a fighting spirit. The whole of Russia at that time was in a turmoil. Bolshevism was beginning, and the Germans were sweeping up the Russian ships and defences as if they were empty. The Russian Naval commander-in-chief went in person to assist in the defence of the Gulf of Riga. When he and his staff arrived at Hapsal they had to walk seven *versts* to Rogikoul, as the railway was on strike for vodka!

The Baltic submarine flotilla vanished with the collapse of Russia, but it had made a great name for itself. Even during the nightmare of revolutionary lunacy that preceded the end, it was looked on by all the Russians as the one straightforward and efficient force that remained. The lowest as well as the highest respected it as the symbol of honesty and corn-age. During its career it had caused the greatest annoyance to the enemy, on occasions holding up and stopping practically all traffic from Germany to Sweden in enemy ships. The following extracts show the way some of the work was done:—

'E 9' (Commander Horton), *October 18th*, 1916, 5.50 p.m.:

Chased steamer and ordered her to stop by International Code and by firing maxim ahead of her. She proved to be the German ship *Soderham* of Hamburg. Boarding party went aboard and told crew to abandon ship, then opened up sea-cocks and exploded demolition charges.

At 7.15 p.m. stopped a ship with flashing lamp and maxim. She was the *Pernambuco* of the Hamburg South American Line—from Lulea to Stettin with iron ore (3500 tons). Sent crew off in boats and sank her. Her chief officer stated her to be of 7000 tons. 6.55 a.m.:

Chased, boarded, and sank the *Johannes Russ* of Hamburg—same routine as previously. 10.47 a.m.: Hove to the German ship *Dal Alfven*, and ordered her to abandon ship. A destroyer was with her, and approached me at speed. It was impossible to discover her nationality end-on, so dived and watched her. She proved to be the Swedish destroyer *Wale*. She took *Dal Alfven*'s crew on board from their boats. Rose and closed *Wale*. Following conversation ensued:—

"*Wale*. 'You are in Swedish neutral waters.'

"'E 9.' 'I make myself six miles from land.'

"*Wale*. 'I make you five.'

"'E 9.' 'Neutral limit is three miles—please stand clear while I sink this ship.'

"11.24 a.m.: Fired stern tube *at Dal Alfven*. *Wale* was 100 yards on our beam. Torpedo ran well and vessel sank in two minutes."

"E 19" (Commander Cromie) was at sea also at this time:—

October 3rd, 5.30 p.m.: Stopped German merchant-man. She would not obey the signal until I hit her with a shell amidships—then she abandoned ship. Put five shot-holes in her water-line, and left her on a lee shore. Weather getting worse.

October 10th: Sea rough with rain squalls. Stopped German

ship *Lulea*. Made crew abandon ship and then sank her.

October 11th: Sank *Walter Leonhardt* of Hamburg. Crew taken aboard Swedish steamer. Then sank *Gutrune*, carrying iron ore to Hamburg. At 4.55 p.m., stopped and sank *Director Rippenhagen*, carrying magnetic ore to Nordenheim. Put the crew aboard Swedish steamer *Martha*. 6.30 p.m.: Sank the *Nicomedia*, carrying iron ore to Hamburg. Crew pulled ashore.

Stopped the *Nike*. This ship requiring further investigation, I put a prize crew on board and sent her to Revel. Her captain informed me that twenty German ships, laden with iron ore, are stopped at Lulea, waiting for escort.

On November 2nd "E 19" was on the traffic route again and sank the *Ruomi* of Hamburg. (The work being done by these boats was the same as the Germans were doing to us, but if the Germans had carried out their work with the same decency and care for the lives of the non-combatants they would be receiving far more consideration and respect from us now.) The enemy had now started to protect their traffic lane, and they sent out a cruiser to drive the E boats away.

"E 19" continues (November 7th, 1.45 p.m.):—

Fired starboard beam tube 1100 yards' range, hitting her forward on starboard side. The cruiser (*Ancona* class) swung round and stopped. At 1.55 p.m. fired stern tube at 1200 yards. Torpedo hit just abaft main-mast, and after-magazine blew up. Three minutes later there was no sign of her.

The German ships torpedoed in the Baltic seem, to have had touchy magazines. Commander Goodhart (E 8) met the *Prinz Adalbert* on October 23rd, 1915. She was zigzagging slightly and going 15 knots, with two destroyers zigzagging ahead as a screen. The torpedo was fired at the fore-bridge as she passed, and—

Observed very vivid flash of explosion along water-line at point of aim. This was immediately followed by a very heavy concussion, and the entire ship was completely hidden by a huge column of thick grey smoke—fore magazine having evidently been exploded by torpedo. As many portions of the ship were observed to be falling in the water all round, I proceeded to 50 feet depth.

The range of this shot was about 1300 yards. This comparatively long distance was fortunate, as the resultant explosion would have probably caused a terrific shock to E 8 had she happened to fire from loser.

The E boats in the Baltic came from Harwich *via* the Sound. It sounds simple, but it was a remarkably difficult and dangerous trip. For six miles in the narrows it is too shallow for a submarine to submerge. The boats had to trim down and go along with their conning-towers showing and their keels bumping along the rocky bottom. The traffic—both neutral and enemy—was so thick that it was not so much a question of avoiding being seen, as of actually avoiding collision. A maze of moving and fixed lights, searchlights, star-shells, and attempts to ram made up a nightmare of navigational difficulties to add to the normal anxiety of passing through thick traffic in a narrow channel. It was really a marvel that any boats got through safely at all.

3

Throughout this history I am giving selections from despatches of typical "contacts" with the enemy, or of those which describe exciting incidents on patrol; but I don't want to give the idea that submarine patrol work was one whirl of gaiety, and that a boat had only to go to sea in order to find a target. The facts are very different. A boat might do a matter of twenty trips without meeting any kind of chance at an enemy, and I suppose that each boat averaged two to three thousand miles of diving between chances. The following description of routine in a patrol boat must stand for four years of blank days in the North Sea, Atlantic, or Mediterranean:—

The boat dives at dawn, and, the trim correct and the captain satisfied, the order is given to "fall out all but diving hands." One officer remains at the periscope, while the remainder and the majority of the crew move off to their sleeping billets and he down. When not on watch it is customary for everybody to sleep, read, and eat all the time; this is to conserve the stock of air in the boat. Oxygen is not carried, but "purifiers" are. The air in the hull of the boat is, however, ample for a long day's dive, and except when kept down by accident or the machinations of the enemy there is no necessity to renew it.

It is kept on the move, however, by ordinary circulating fans, which produce a general draught and disturbance of the halos of bad air around each man's head, and this keeping of the air moving makes a great difference—in fact, with no fans running a match fails to burn after nine hours' diving; with all fans circulating a match can be lit after a dive of from fourteen to eighteen hours. Why this is, I don't know. If any work is done while diving (such as reloading of tubes or repairing of damage) the air is used more rapidly—in fact, extraordinarily quickly.

When no work is being done, but only the usual day's dive has been carried out, there is a slight increase in rate of respiration among the hands on watch, with a slighter rise in rate of pulse. But as soon as one attempts to do anything, such as lifting weights or making a speech to the crew on the subject of their crimes, one finds it necessary to breathe heavily and quickly; and in fact, in the case of the speech, only a few minutes' harangue would be possible towards the end of a day.

Officers do not keep watch at the periscope for more than a couple of hours at a time—it is bad for the eyes and bad for the temper; the deadly monotony of shuffling slowly round while stooping to stare at a perfectly blank and usually misty horizon is the worst part of a patrol. The periscope work makes one sleepy also. Submarine officers sleep a lot; the work is dull and sleep passes the time. One gets tired of reading, although one certainly reads an extraordinary amount.

A succession of blank uneventful trips is good for education, however; somebody once said that the book to be cast away on a desert island with was Gibbons' *Roman Empire*. I have known heavier books than that to be worked through on patrol—even to weighty tomes on Constitutional History. The sailors also read, sleep, and eat continuously. A few hands keep watch on the hydroplane wheels, the pumps, and the motors; the rest take it easy. They study such periodicals as one finds on the counters of small tobacconists' shops, and in addition they borrow and read intelligently the more abstruse literature from their officers' library.

There is not much cooking done while diving. Cooking is done in electric ovens and boilers, but it is usual to do what work is necessary with these when the boats are charging batteries on the surface. Cooking when submerged uses oxygen, makes smells, and expends battery power, and is discouraged. Cold meals are the rule, and submarine people cannot complain of being underfed, as there is a special supply for them of bottled fruits and other extras to obviate the dangers of illness to men living without exercise or fresh air in such confined quarters. On the whole, the crews keep healthy and fit, but there has been a good deal of illness and also eye-strain among the officers during the war.

I have said that while one officer is on watch at the periscope the others sleep or read. It is remarkable, however, how awake they are to certain sounds or happenings. An officer may take some minutes to rouse when called for his spell on watch, but if instead of the gentle shaking of the messenger he felt a change of inclination of the boat, or a new vibratory note from the motors, or if he felt by the cessation of rolling that the boat was sinking, he would be awake in a flash.

The human brain seems to keep one technical department always on watch, and it misses nothing. A boat patrolling in a slight swell keeps up a gentle roll at periscope depth, and all the time one hears the rattle and click of the shafting as the fore and aft hydroplanes are worked to keep her at her depth-line. If, for instance, she meets a stratum of fresh water, she will begin to sink; the hydroplanes will be worked up to "hard-a-rise" and left there, with the boat inclined up and trying to climb. The officer at the periscope will order a tank to be partially emptied and will increase speed on the motors to help her climb up again.

As she goes down the rolling will cease, and the silence of the hydroplane shafts, the hum of the motors, and the angle of the boat will tell every sleeper at once exactly what is happening; some of them could probably tell the actual depth the boat had got down to without looking at the gauge. In the same way when on passage on the surface a change of note in the roar of the Diesel engines will wake all hands—it might mean something important.

When on the surface, there is one sound which wakes everybody without any exception—and that is the electric alarm horn. It makes a dry blaring noise which is unmistakable, and in view of the fact that it may be the preliminary to the loss of the boat, it interests all hands very intimately. There is always the feeling, especially if it is dark, that the officer on watch may have rung it too late, and that before the boat can be forced under a destroyer stem may come crashing through the pressure hull.

A submarine hates being on the surface—at least, a patrol submarine does. She has to come up to recharge her batteries or to "make a passage." It must be reiterated that a submarine is fairly fast and of long radius on the surface, and of slow speed and low capacity submerged. It will be understood that a boat is in an anxious position if she has been diving long and her battery is low when she is near enemy patrols. She has got to come up and charge again, and while charging a low battery she is rather helpless. Every weapon has its weak point, and a knowledge of where the weakness lies means a chance to the opponent.

Neither side had any submarines present at the Battle of Jutland, for the simple reason that neither side had at that time any boats fast enough to cruise with the Fleet and so arrive in time at a tactical rendezvous. One boat did arrive at the scene of battle next day—a homeward-bound U-boat who knew nothing of what had happened; she passed through an area of water which was covered with corpses, wreckage, and debris, and which was occasion-ally marked by the ends of sunken ships standing up above the surface. She cruised about, wondering, for a time, and then hurried on into harbour.

If, however, there had been another fleet action during the war, the fast submarine would have been represented in it. The Germans never built anything like our K class boats, and so the war test of the type would have been carried out by us only. Tests in practice had given such good results that the reluctance of the enemy to repeat the Jutland experiment was very disappointing to the K-boat officers, who had two years of waiting for their one chance—a chance which never arrived.

A submarine of 2600 tons cannot throw up her tail and slip under in a few seconds as an E boat can do—she must be taken under with due respect for her great length and size, and she cannot therefore be used on the usual Bight patrols. She is built and designed for battle only, and the type, apart from a few "incidents "with enemy submarines while employed on scouting patrols, had to share the fate of the Grand Fleet battleships which never got a fair chance at the enemy. The building of these boats, however, showed us that the big submarine was a working possibility. We designed and built them to a certain specification, and they showed they could improve on that specification in practice, and they gave most valuable data for future design.

There is, at any rate, one point on which prophecy as to the future of submarines (if they are allowed by International Law to continue to develop) is safe: at present a boat has to travel submerged by electric power, because that is the only form of propulsion we know which does not consume air. When an engine arrives which can propel a boat under water by abstracting the necessary oxygen from the surrounding sea, we will have made the submersible a commercial proposition.

A properly stream-fined body moves faster under than on the surface of water, and with a submersible internal combustion engine there would be in all probability a doubling of the speed of ships. That such a type of engine will come there is little doubt, and when it is remembered that water is a far cheaper protection from shells than is armour-plate, a field for prophecy is opened which is much too big and tempting to venture into here.

Whatever happens, the German policy of torpedoing merchant ships without warning must be made not only illegal, but unsafe for a nation adopting it; the use of this weapon by the enemy has made the word "submarine" one of reproach; the submarine personnel of every allied navy feels that an honourable weapon has, on its first appearance in a great sea war, had its name degraded by a section of its users. If these notes of mine serve no other purpose, they will at any rate do something towards differentiating between the submarine and the U-boat. If the name of the weapon is to become a term of reproach, it is better to particularise and to spare the honour of the Allied Navies.

I am going to relate an incident which occurred during the war. It was not in the presence of the enemy, and so there is little direct connection between it and a War History. But it is illustrative of the ideas of the Submarine Service in that it evoked little comment among the Flotillas, the standard shown by the personnel being considered to be normal, and in accordance with accepted practice.

Submarine "C 12" was under way in the Humber; her main driving motors failed, and before the fault could be remedied or anchors let go, she was carried by the strong ebb-tide against the bows of destroyers which were lying at the Eastern Jetty at Immingham, and badly holed. Most of the crew and the first lieutenant (Lieutenant Sullivan) were below at the time, while the captain (Lieutenant Manley) was on deck.

Seeing that the boat was sinking fast, Lieutenant Manley ordered all hands on deck. They hurried up, the first lieutenant remaining below. The water was pouring in over the electric batteries, causing heavy chlorine fumes to be given off. The boat was on the verge of sinking when, the last man being up, Lieutenant Manley went below, closing the conning-tower lid after him. The boat then went to the bottom, with both officers inside her. Finding, however, that nothing could be done owing to the extent of the damage, the chlorine gas, and the weight of water entering, these officers entered the conning-tower, closing the lower door after them. They then flooded the conning-tower and, lifting the upper door, swam to the surface, reporting that nothing could now be done without salvage plant to lift the boat.

War produces a lot of incidents of a note-worthy kind, but work in submarines produces similar incidents under peace conditions also, because the Service is always at war with its constant enemy—the sea. The boats have small buoyancy, and a leak is a dangerous thing; they are very vulnerable to the ram, and even in peace man-oeuvres before the war we lost six boats from collisions either on the surface or diving.

During the war we lost 61 boats, of which seven were blown up without losses in personnel—these being the boats of the Baltic Flotilla. 20 were lost from a cause unknown. In other words, they went on patrol, and nothing more was heard of them.

The enemy have no knowledge of their fate, and there were no survivors from them. Their loss was probably due to their striking mines.

Five were sunk by enemy submarines (one of them—"E 20"—in the Sea of Marmora).

Three were sunk while entering the Dardanelles, and one by gun-fire in the Marmora.

Four were sunk by mines off our own coasts. Three were wrecked on neutral coasts, one in the Baltic, and one on our own coast.

Two were sunk by air bombs. Seven were sunk by collision.

Three were sunk in error by gun or ram by our own side. One sank in harbour, one sank on trials, one was sunk by gun-fire after sinking a German destroyer off the Bight, and "C 3" blew herself up on St George's Day against the Mole at Zeebrugge.

The losses were heavy, but were not incurred uselessly. The boats were the outposts of the Fleet, and, however great the losses, they could never have equalled those the bigger ships would have had to endure had they been given the same patrols to perform. Looking at the above list, one can see that the majority of the losses were due to mines. Losses by direct contact with the enemy were infrequent. This, of course, is because only a Fleet holding command of the sea can institute regular anti-submarine methods and patrols.

Our boats were working in and around the Bight, and were taking the risks of mine-fields all the time. The five wrecks show that navigational difficulties are increased in war-time. This was found also by surface vessels. The Dardanelles took their toll; it was easy to do damage to traffic in the Marmora from a well-trained submarine, but getting in and out of the Narrows was no simple matter.

Of the two sunk by air bombs, one was alongside in harbour, and the other was destroyed by an Allied aircraft which mistook her for a U-boat; the submarine could have easily dived and avoided attack, but was under the impression her unfortunate opponent was only closing in order to make signals. The three others sunk in error by our own side show that a submarine's risks are great even on her own coast, and that methods of identification can never be perfected. The enemy suffered more than we did from errors. They had several clashes between their own destroyers: on June 1 (the morning after Jutland) the *Stettin* was fired on by the whole of their 2nd Battle Squadron; while one U-boat in 1914 successfully stalked and torpedoed another (U 5), thinking it was one of our own.

CHAPTER 6

Adventures, Losses & Escapes

I have mentioned the fact that Submarine "A E 2" (Lieutenant-Commander Stoker) was the first boat to get into the Sea of Marmora. Her experience is worth relating, especially in view of the fact that she was an Australian Navy boat, and that her trip was made simultaneously with the Gallipoli landing.

She entered the Straits at 2.30 a.m. on 25th April 1915, and continued upon the surface till, being fired on from the northern shore, she dived at 4.30 a.m., and proceeded at 70 feet depth through the mine-field. Her despatches say:—

> During the ensuing half-hour or so the scraping of wires against the vessel's sides was almost continuous, and on two occasions something caught up forward and continued to knock for some considerable time before breaking loose and scraping away aft.

Off Chanak she torpedoed a small Turkish gunboat in passing, and dodged the stem of a torpedo-boat that attempted to ram the periscope. "A E 2" then ran aground (her compass having developed defects) under the guns of Fort Anatoli Mejidieh. She got off, and proceeded on at 90 feet, till she ran aground again on the Gallipoli shore for five minutes. This second bump damaged the hull somewhat. She got off and went on, pursued by all the miscellaneous small craft of the Narrows, all of them firing at and trying to ram her periscope.

At 8.30 a.m., the pursuit being close, she intentionally ran aground on the Asiatic shore to wait, at a depth of 80 feet, till the chase should have passed on overhead. She waited there, listening to the propellers passing to and fro, until 9 p.m., when she rose and found nothing in sight. At 4 a.m. on the 26th she went on, having charged up her batteries and unsuccessfully attacked two unknown men-of-war (one of them probably the battleship *Hairedin Barbarossa*) near Gallipoli. At 9 a.m. she entered the Sea of Marmora. Unfortunately, "A E 2" carried no gun, and had to rely on her torpedo armament, which at 9.30 a.m. failed her when she endeavoured to sink a transport—one of four coming towards the Peninsula.

On 27th April she had more bad luck with torpedoes, and another transport (escorted by a destroyer screen) escaped her. On the 28th another torpedo failed to hit a small ship convoyed by two T.B.D.'s, and in the evening her sixth torpedo missed on "two men-of-war approaching at high speed from westward." On the 29th, being chased by torpedo-boats and gunboats, she was forced to fire a chance shot in order to discourage the pursuit. The torpedo missed a yard ahead of a gunboat, and "pursuit then ceased." In the evening she met "E 14" at a rendezvous, the latter boat having followed her up the Straits. On the 30th, "A E 2" met her end:—

10.30 a.m.: Boat's bow suddenly rose, and boat broke surface about one mile from T.B. Blew water forward, but could not get boat to dive. Torpedo-boat got very close, firing, and a gunboat from Artaki Bay began firing at a range of about three miles; flooded a forward tank, when boat suddenly took a big inclination down by bows and dived rapidly. The 100-feet depth-line was quickly reached and passed. Went full speed astern and commenced to blow main ballast.

After some interval boat came back to 100-feet depth, so re-flooded and went ahead, but boat broke surface stern first. "Within a few seconds the shots fired holed the engine-room in three places. Owing to the great inclination down by the bow it was impossible to see the torpedo-boat through the periscope, and I considered that any attempt to ram her would be useless. I therefore blew main ballast, and ordered all hands on deck. Assisted by Lieutenant Haggard, I then opened the tanks to flood and went on deck. The boat sank in a few minutes. . . .

All the officers and men were saved, being picked out of the water by the Turkish torpedo-boat after "A E 2" had sunk. A lot of trips were made by submarines up the Sea of Marmora, but it was not all child's play inside or on the way up. "E 15" and "E 14" were lost in the Straits, "E 20" was torpedoed by a U-boat when off Constantinople, and "E 7" was sunk in the Chanak nets.

As was published at the time, submarine "E 13" was lost on the 18th September 1915, on Saltholm, Denmark. As a matter of fact her loss with part of the crew was part of the price paid by the Navy for the passage of E boats into the Baltic. "E 13" was bound for Libau *via* the Sound, and was wrecked owing to a defective compass. She was doubtful enough of the compass's accuracy for such narrow and intricate waters to have eased to 250 evolutions and to have stopped one engine when she grounded on the S.E. end of Saltholm, striking all along her length on shelving rocky bottom.

She blew all tanks and began operations to get away. At 5 a.m. a Danish torpedo-boat arrived and communicated, stating that "E 13" had twenty-four hours to get herself away in, but that no assistance could be given her. . . . Then a German destroyer arrived and remained watching until two Danish torpedo-boats approached, when she left. At 9 a.m. "E 13" was still trying to move, and three Danish torpedo-boats were anchored watching her; then came two German destroyers.

At half a mile range the leading enemy hoisted a signal and blew her syren. Before the signal could be read she was three hundred yards away, at which range she fired a torpedo and opened fire with all guns. "E 13," hit all over, caught fire at once, and Commander Layton ordered the crew to abandon ship, telling them to take to the water and scatter as much as possible, the German fire being "Man-killing," *i.e.* with shrapnel and machine-gun.

The Danish torpedo-boats at once got out their boats, and one torpedo-boat steamed in between the Germans and their target—this action causing the Germans to cease fire. The Germans then withdrew, having killed fifteen officers and men of "E 13" in the water. The submarine was hit about fourteen times by four-inch shells and by many of smaller calibre; she was completely destroyed. The officers and men saved were taken aboard the Danish flagship and treated with the utmost kindness. I will not comment on this incident.

Commander Layton escaped from his prison in Denmark, and returned safely to command another submarine.

I must record here the account of the escape of Stoker Petty Officer William Brown. It was an extraordinary experience for any man, but I must again point out that the submarine sailor is, in his training and sense, something out of the common.

The submarine Brown was in was acting as "target" for other boats which were practising attacks on her as training for actual war attacks on U-boats at sea. The exercising area was just off Harwich, and the "target" was running a straight course along it, looking out for the periscope of the attacker. Suddenly the periscope appeared—50 yards on the bow and travelling fast; a collision was inevitable.

The attacker's conning-tower was smashed, and she sank at once with all hands. The captain of the "target" was on the bridge, and receiving a report that his own boat was sinking fast, he called all hands on deck. Petty Officer Brown did not apparently hear the order, and with two other men (a stoker and engine-room artificer) went down with the boat.

The conning-tower lid being open as she sank, the stoker and artificer who were in the midship compartment waited a few seconds in a pocket of air near the conning-tower ladder, and then dived for it, swimming through the boat till the gleam of brighter water showed overhead, then rising up through sixty-five feet till they gained the surface. Brown had taken shelter in the engine-room, closing the door after him. His own account of the incident is quite clear, though perhaps a little technical.

> Something was heard to come in contact with the bottom of the boat forward, twice in quick succession. Immediately after the engine-room telegraph rang to 'out-clutches.' I took out the port clutch and closed the muffler valve—then it was reported that the ship was making water. I proceeded forward to ascertain the position of the leak, and came to the conclusion she was holed down low.
> My first impulse was to close the lower door of the conning-tower. At this point the chief engine-room artificer inquired if all hands were out of the engine-room. I replied I would find out. On going aft I found one man coming forward, and I ordered him to put his life-belt on, keep his head, and wait his turn at the conning-tower hatch. Finding there was nobody else aft, I came forward and put on a life-belt and closed the valve on the air trunk through the engine-room bulkhead—then water began to come down through the conning-tower hatch and the boat took a dip forward. . . .

From the collision to this point was actually about 90 seconds. Brown leaves the impression in one's mind that he spent part of this time "tidying up" and generally giving a final polish to his department before leaving (perhaps he did):—

> I went aft and shouted to the hands forward to come aft to the engine-room. There was no response. The midship compartment was in darkness and partly flooded. Chlorine gas began to come through. I closed the engine-room door and began to unscrew the clips of the torpedo hatch above me. At this juncture the engine-room was in complete darkness, with the exception of the port pilot-lamp, which was burning through 'earth.' The water was slowly rising in the engine-room through the voice-pipes, which I had left open to relieve the pressure on the bulkhead door.

I then proceeded to disconnect the torpedo hatch from its gearing, which meant the removal of two split pins and two pins from the links. Before the fore-most one could be removed, however, I had to unship the strongback and wait till there was sufficient pressure in the boat to ease the hatch off the strong-back. . . .

It all sounds so very simple, but the man misses out a lot. It was almost pitch-dark. He was working on top of the engines of a nearly full submarine which had gone to the bottom. He was half-submerged in electrically-charged water, and chlorine gas was coming in through the voice-pipes from the batteries. The hatch he was trying to open was very heavy—well screwed down—and was over his head in a difficult position to reach.

The heat at this time was excessive, therefore I rested awhile and considered the best means of flooding the engine-room, and eventually came to the conclusion that the best way was to flood through the stern tube or the weed-trap of the circulating system, or by dropping the exhaust and induction valves and opening the muffler-valve. I tried the stern tube first, but could neither open the stern-cap nor rear door.

Then I came forward again. Whilst passing the switch-boards I received several shocks. I tried to open the weed-trap of the circulating inlet, but it was in an awkward posi-tion, and with water coming over the top of me I could not ease back the butterfly-nuts. So proceeded forward again and opened muffler-valve, also the test-cocks on the group exhaust-valves; tried them and found water was coming in. Then I climbed on top of the engines under-neath the torpedo hatch and unshipped the strongback, drawing the pin out of the link with a spanner that I had with me. In order to flood the boat completely I opened the scuttle in the engine-room bulkhead.

Chlorine gas came in as well as water. I tried three times to lift the torpedo hatch, but each time could only open it half-way, and each time air rushed out through it and the hatch fell down again. I clipped the hatch again, having to dive down to fetch the clip-bolts, and as the pressure increased again, I knocked off the clips. The hatch flew open, but not enough to let me out.

I tried to lift it again with my shoulder, but it descended on my hand. I managed to raise the hatch sufficiently to clear my hand and let it down again. Then I flooded the boat rapidly through the deadlight till the water came to the level of the coaming. I was then able to raise the hatch and come to the surface. . . .

To put the case from the point of view of the destroyer lying above the scene of the collision, bubbles and gouts of oil and gas came up for an hour and a half after the boat had sunk. Then a man appeared swimming. He wore an air-belt, he had a smashed hand and was very done, but was full of information for the salvage party with reference to the state of the boat he had just left, such as which valves, doors, etc., were open and which were closed.

During the war the High Sea Fleet was seldom seen by any ships, submersible or otherwise, but "E 23" (Lieutenant-Commander Turner) had a very good view of them on 19th August 1916.

At three o'clock in the morning, in clear weather, cloudy with no moon, she saw ships steering west by Borkum Riff. She got her tubes ready and stood in to attack on the surface. As she closed, trimmed half-down, and with every one keyed up for the shot, she saw the German battle-cruisers go by, their destroyer screen passing her at dangerously close range. As the destroyer wash dashed against the conning-tower and the resultant gleam of phosphorus indicated her presence to the enemy, she fired a beam tube at the *Sedylitz*, the leading ship.

As she did so the *Seydlitz* opened on her with her secondary battery at 800 yards' range. "E 23" dived and ran down to the bottom in 140 feet to reload. The *Seydlitz* must have dodged as the boat fired, and the torpedo missed. At 3.30 a.m. "E 23" rose and saw smoke to the south-east. She attacked, diving at full speed, and made out eight battleships in single line ahead with destroyers on either bow of each ship and Zeppelins overhead. This was the *König* and *Kaiser* class squadron following the battle-cruisers. As they were obviously going to pass her at long range, "E 23" gave them one chance torpedo at 4000 to 5000 yards' range without success, and turned her attention to eight more battleships astern of them—*viz.*, four *Heligoland* class, four *Nassau* class, with one Zeppelin, and a destroyer screen. She fired two torpedoes at the rear ship (the *Westfalen*), hitting her with one, and making a hole 45 feet by 14 feet along her side.

The destroyers turned to ram, but "E 23" was at 90 feet by the time they arrived overhead. As their propellers passed she came to periscope depth again and saw the *Westfalen* listing to starboard with her speed reduced. The damaged ship made an effort to follow her consorts, while the submarine dived westward after her; but her consorts were not waiting for lame ducks, and they had passed on at 18 knots.

The big ship turned, and with five destroyers guarding her, came back towards harbour. "E 23" fired again, and this time as she hurried down to 90 feet after the shot, heard depth-charges exploding after her. Whether she hit with the last shot or not is doubtful. In the midst of the depth-charges it is impossible to differentiate and locate a torpedo explosion. But the *Westfalen* was got home and into dock.

As soon as the chase had ceased, "E 23" rose and signalled the news of the High Sea Fleet's venture to the Grand Fleet, but on the latter's approach the enemy had turned back from the mouth of the Bight and passed home by the Northern Channel. During the attack on the Fleet "E 23" had a perfect view in clear weather of all the ships, and was able to note all funnel bands and distinctive markings on them, and to recognise each unit of the great Armada as it crossed the periscope field.

The big "K" class submarines were used for scouting patrols in 1917 and 1918. This was not because we were short of boats, but because it was known that if boats don't get in sea-time they tend to become inefficient—also, perhaps it was known that we would have plenty of warning from the Intelligence Department if the High Sea Fleet moved, and so could call the "K's" home to refill with oil in readiness if a fleet action was likely. The "K" patrols were on lines between the Bight and our coast which enemy raiders or mine-layers would be likely to cross if they came out.

Except for practice dives at dawn and evening, the boats stayed on the surface all the time, zigzagging up and down their patrol lines at 17 knots. Apart from occasional U-boats or our own ships nothing was seen, and the work done was like most of the patrol work of the war—very dull, but useful and necessary. The boats, however, were able to test their own behaviour in bad weather on several occasions, with the result that weak points could be eliminated or strengthened, and the design modified and made more seaworthy. A K boat in a gale is a very handsome ship, her smooth run and fine lines slide the seas off very prettily, and if her speed is eased to suit the length of the sea she rides like a cruiser.

It is true that she is not comfortable in bad weather: in the boiler-room the stokers have to wear oilskins because of the water pouring down from the vents overhead, and big seas sometimes come down the funnels, causing "flashing-back" and scalding; the water tumbles down the conning-tower hatch, splashing off the control-room deck and causing "earths" on adjacent switchboards, with the result that men going up and down the conning-tower ladder are greeted with shocks as soon as they grasp the rungs.

They have a quick destroyer-like roll, and, unless going slow, they have a trick of neglecting to lift occasionally when meeting a head sea; but they are really safe sea-boats, and if trim and speed are correctly adjusted, far more comfortable in bad weather than destroyers are. Their great advantage is in their lines, for a smooth-run hull with no obstructions deflects, instead of holding, the water.

All submarines are pretty wet in a head sea, for they are heavy vessels with little buoyancy, and do not lift in time to the waves, so that a passage to windward in an E boat, for instance, is for the men on the bridge one long cold bath, especially in the short breaking seas of the Dogger, when a boat goes butting into everything as it comes without troubling to rise to it. I have not figures to refer to, but can at any rate remember one captain, one first lieutenant, and two seamen being lost overboard at different times from boats on passage in North Sea gales during the war.

The German cargo submarine *Deutschland* was considerably endangered on her voyage to America by the big Atlantic seas tumbling down her conning-tower: it is considered in Germany that the loss of the *Bremen* on her first voyage was due to something of the sort—that the boat put her nose into a head sea, and filled before her hatch could be shut down, or she could lift again in the next hollow. In the North Atlantic there may be 500 yards of trough between the wave-crests in a gale, and a heavy submarine running down the slope would be liable to bury herself in the next great hill of water as it met her.

Many incidents must have occurred during the war of which we have now no record. The boats which were lost in the Bight "from causes unknown" may have been on their patrol billets for some time before meeting their end, and what they did and what they saw will never be known. On at least one occasion the veil has been lifted: "L 10" (Lieutenant-Commander White-house) was known to have been sunk by German destroyers in October last; it was after the Armistice that we heard that she had first sunk a German destroyer, "S 33," and had then herself been destroyed by the remainder of the flotilla.

When we get a German account of the war at sea we may find in it here and there a belated piece of news of a missing E boat. It is, however, believed that the enemy destroyed most of his records and despatches during the Revolution, in order to prevent what would have been, from his point of view, premature publication.

In August 1916, submarine "E 16" (Lieutenant-Commander Duff-Dunbar) was lost in the Bight. She was proceeding to a billet in the enemy northern swept channel, and "E 38" was following her at about seven miles distance. Seeing smoke on the horizon ahead, "E 38" dived, but could not get within range of the enemy ships (which are known to have been cruisers). She saw, however, splashes rise from the water near the ships as if they were firing at something, and this is confirmed by enemy reports that on that day they fired at a periscope attacking them. Firing at a periscope does not at all imply that the fire has damaged the boat, but from a vague statement by a German officer of the boat being "blown up" by the gunfire, one can surmise that "E 16" struck a mine while attacking. Her captain was an officer who stood very high in his contemporaries' estimation, in addition to being highly thought of by his seniors, and the approval of equals is harder to earn than that of one's seniors.

He had, in December 1915, torpedoed and sunk an enemy net-layer off the Western Ems. E boats having been seen by the enemy off this river, they sent out a 3000-ton auxiliary to lay anti-submarine nets on the billet. The ship was escorted by four trawlers, a torpedo-boat, a small sloop, and several tugs and other small craft, but apart from the fact that there is Scriptural instruction against laying snares in sight of the bird, the enemy should have realised that an escort screen is no protection against a determined attack. "E 16" approached the screen, the units of which were zigzagging round the ship; she had to cut things fine, as the units were numerous, and the intervals between them small. Her periscope crossed the stern of an armed trawler at a range of fifty yards, and looking in the eyepiece Duff-Dunbar saw a sailor at the trawler's stern point at him, stabbing his finger at the six inches of thin tube that passed, and opening his mouth widely in what was guessed to be a volume of Teutonic sound.

Two torpedoes were fired, while the escort charged and shouted and blew syrens, but the target had a section of net over the stern on its way out, and she was practically stopped and helpless; she sank in twelve minutes amidst a scene of great excitement. Three torpedo-boats and four trawlers hunted and swept for "E 16" for four hours, but she watched the proceedings from some distance off through her periscope, and in view of the high speed and constant alterations of course used by the torpedo-boats, refrained from joining in with further torpedo practice. Submarine "E 38," just mentioned, met the High Sea Fleet on the 19th October 1916.

Friday 13th: Left Harwich in execution of previous orders.

14th: Started diving patrol.

15th:Violent south-westerly gale, and a very heavy sea.

16th: Strong W.N.W. gale. High confused sea.

17th: Light N.W. wind. Moderate swell.

18th: Fine weather.

19th: 6.22 a.m. sighted funnels and masts of heavy ships to the E.N.E. . . .

I have put that extract in to show, firstly, how dull a patrol normally is, and, secondly, how the boats have to wait on their billets at all times and in all weather, while the enemy comes to sea at his convenience when it is nice and calm. "E 38" dived at full speed to attack, but could not get within range of the leading squadron, which was composed of battle-cruisers and destroyers, and which was zigzagging at high speed. Then came two light cruisers, at one of which Lieutenant-Commander Jessop fired but missed at 600 yards. On raising his periscope again he "observed destroyers zigzagging at high speed in all directions."

Then came the battle Fleet, which passed out of range, and then a light cruiser—the *München*—with the usual screen of destroyers zigzagging each side of her. Allowing her a speed of 22 knots, "E 38" torpedoed her abreast the foremost funnel, filling the whole of the forward boiler-room with water and damaging her severely. The weather being calm and the bulkheads sound, the ship was safely got into harbour by the Germans. Two boats were lost on the Dutch coast in 1916 and the crews interned.

The first was "E 17," on the 6th January. She was carried in by an exceptional set of water into the Texel when steering for

Terschelling. She pounded and hammered on the banks in a breaking sea till she was strained, leaking and damaged; then she got off and started back on the surface to Harwich.

An unfortunate incident then betrayed her. She met a Dutch cruiser, which approached in such a way that her colours were not visible, and (being at practice gun stations) with her guns swinging in "E 17's" direction. Lieutenant-Commander Moncrieffe very naturally took her for an enemy and dived. As soon as the boat was under, the pounding she had received on the shoal showed its full effect. She began to fill, and the water reaching her battery and chlorine fumes being emitted, she had to be hastily brought to the surface.

Still under the impression that the cruiser was German, Lieutenant-Commander Moncrieffe sank his boat. It was the actual fact that the boat was forced to dive that made her past salving: if she had been able to continue her voyage to England on the surface she would probably—given good weather and hard pumping—have arrived home.

The second boat, "H 6," ran ashore in misty weather on Schiermonnikoog—well in the Bight. She went hard on to the shoals and lay with a big list two and a half miles from the lighthouse. She sent a wireless signal to Captain Waistell, commanding the Flotilla, who was at sea superintending the operations of Ins boats in the T.B.D. *Firedrake*. Captain Waistell hurried to the spot, but realised that in such a position (close to enemy harbours) it would be impossible to carry out salvage operations.

He decided, however, to send a motor-boat in with orders to "H 6" to send off the confidential books and the more highly trained ratings of the crew—her captain with the remaining hands staying to see to her salvage and internment. This was done, though the operation took over two hours—an anxious time for all concerned. The boat was salved by the Dutch, and subsequently disposed of by us to their Government.

The enemy, of course, lost several boats by grounding and subsequent surrender on our coasts. The Goodwins, the Shipwash, and the French shoals were the end of some boats, and others were certainly damaged and weakened by contact with outlying parts of these islands. The case of "U-C 5" will be remembered, as she was salved and taken up the Thames to be shown to the public. She was herded on to the Shipwash shoal off Harwich by destroyers, and she then surrendered to H.M.S. *Firedrake* after touching off demolition charges against her mining-room bulkhead. The mines did not go off, and the boat remained more or less undamaged by the explosions. Lieutenant Patterson, torpedo-lieutenant of the 8th Submarine Flotilla, then dived into her as she lay half-submerged and removed the detonator plugs of her mines. For this act he was later decorated. U-C boats were always laying mines off Harwich, with occasional success; they certainly managed to destroy in this way two of our boats as they left harbour.

Our mine-laying submarines used to return the compliment at Zeebrugge. Perhaps the most exciting mine laid by us was the one which was accidentally let go in the middle of the submarine exercising area off Harwich harbour. The boat that had slipped it reported the fact broadcast, and everybody out near the area, knowing that the unpleasant piece of cargo had functioned correctly, and, with no discrimination between friend or foe, was waiting at its correct depth below the surface for something to hit it, cleared off hurriedly. The sweepers were sent for and the obstruction removed, after which the exercises proceeded as before.

The Germans had some similar incidents which turned out more unpleasantly—at least, from their point of view. On one occasion a half-flotilla of boats were lying alongside their parent ship in Wilhelmshaven. A sailor accidentally let a mine go from the outside boat; the mine was due to become "alive" after a quarter of an hour, and was, owing to the shoal water, already rubbing the keels of the boats.

An instant report by the sailor of what he had done, and a general movement of the boats away, would have saved the situation; but the sailor did not rise to the occasion. His home was in far-distant Hanover, and he started for it and demobilisation as fast as he could run. Punctually to time the mine exploded violently, and the half-flotilla was suddenly reduced in numbers.

The enemy also suffered from a very touchy pistol which they introduced for the war-heads of their torpedoes. It was a very good pistol for service, as it went off un-failingly on contact with our ships, but it had the disadvantage of doing the same thing aboard German submarines if they pitched heavily in a seaway, which made it rather unpopular and led to its modification. This type of torpedo pistol is thought by the Germans to have caused the loss of the light cruiser *Karlsruhe*, which unaccountably blew up off the coast of South America in 1915.

A U-boat was certainly lost in Kiel from this cause, a torpedo having slid forward in the tube until it touched the outer door, when it at once exploded. That sort of case explains why, in night encounters at short range between British and German submarines, our enemies never tried to use the ram; with the same kind of hair-trigger explosives in our tubes we would have been equally cautious.

I want to tell some stories about submarine sailors here, but there are such hundreds of incidents to record that it is impossible to tell many. In despatches of submarine captains describing successes against the enemy, one sees almost every time: "The whole crew having carried out their duties calmly and admirably, it is impossible for me to recommend any particular men for decoration . . ." But I remember an incident near the Hiorns Reef Light Vessel, when a boat approached a suspicious trawler and dived past her to investigate—finding that the suspected gun in the bows was in reality a spar on the capstan, the boat "dipped" to seventy feet to turn away; but owing to the trawler altering course as she did so, dived right into the trawl net and hung up in it.

It seeming extremely probable that the net was a real submarine-catching device, and that the trawler was hostile, it was decided to wait a while before rising, in order that ammunition, etc., might be prepared at the conning-tower foot, and general frightfulness arranged for the expected fight on the surface.

Meanwhile, with her motors stopped, the boat was towed along in the net, taking extraordinary angles every way, and generally acting like a trapped salmon. When ready, the tanks were blown, and the boat rose with a rush, breaking surface in a festoon of net and wires close under the trawler's stern. The gun's crew jumped to their stations, riflemen lay down on the bridge deck, and a petty officer with an axe started to chop away the wires that were holding the boat. It was desirable, owing to the presence of a distant Zeppelin, to get clear and dive again as soon as possible, whether an altercation was necessary with the trawler or not, and so the petty officer was instructed to get a move on.

As a matter of fact, the trawler was Dutch, and hoisted her colours to prove it, so that no shooting was necessary; but the chief feature of the incident was that from his arrival on deck with the axe, to the "plop" of the last wire being cut through five minutes later (when he straightened up, and luridly asked when the shooting was going to begin), the petty officer never looked round or faced to see what kind of enemy he had to engage. He chopped with his back turned, showing a fine lack of curiosity and a strict attention to business. The submarine sailor is really an imperturbable person.

A boat was engaged in attacking a U-boat which had come to the surface half a mile away to charge her batteries, unaware of the presence of the E boat diving past on patrol. The sighting of the enemy, and the call to "action stations," came as the sailor servant was laying the officers' breakfast; the attack, owing to the circles and evolutions of the target, took an hour.

As the E boat turned in on her firing course, her captain lowered the periscope, and steadying his voice to hide his excitement, passed the word: "We'll fire in three minutes—stand by bow tubes"; and at once a voice spoke by his side—a voice confident in the fact that a definite time-interval had at last been mentioned—"Your coffee, sir. Will you have it now? It's getting cold." It is regretted that the captain's placidity was so far short of his subordinate's that he abruptly refused the offer.

The same sailor on one occasion, when acting as officers' cook, quite surpassed himself at dinner by producing a very excellent but mysterious savoury when the boat was a week out on patrol. His tact was not equal to his cooking, however, for on being questioned as to the savoury's ingredients, he explained that "four o' the eggs and the last bit o' cheese went west yesterday, and I didn't like to waste 'em." But then curry-powder will camouflage anything if you use enough.

The submarine sailor is a picked man and a high standard is expected of him. The officers do their best to show him what the standard should be, but he is able to produce examples on his own for the instruction of his messmates. When in July 1918 "C 25" was attacked by five German seaplanes off Harwich, and the captain and all hands on deck were shot down by machine-gun fire, the first lieutenant started up the conning-tower to investigate, and as he came up, Leading-Seaman Barge, the only one alive of four on the bridge, called down to him, "Dive; don't worry about me, I'm done for."

The boat did not dive; she got back to harbour on the surface, but Leading-Seaman Barge was dead five minutes after his last speech—a speech which, thinking it over, appears to be not a bad epitaph.

In 1915 a man well known to the Submarine Service—a Submarine Flotilla Chaplain—went out in "E 4," under Commander Leir, to see for himself how his messmates spent their time on patrol. It is usual in patrol submarines to have as few hands on deck as possible—in fact, nobody is allowed on deck beyond the officer on watch, a lookout, and perhaps one other. On this occasion "E 4," having the chaplain on board, decided to call her crew to prayers on deck while they were on passage to their area, but the crowded state of the bridge a few minutes later was rather a handicap to quick diving when a Zeppelin interrupted the service.

The *padre*, however, had no intention of being a mere passenger, and during the trip he, after a little training, was able to stand his trick on a hydroplane wheel when diving. A survivor from an armed trawler torpedoed by "E 4" was also a grateful guest, and the curious sight might occasionally have been seen of a German prisoner and a naval chaplain sitting on adjacent stools and working the diving-wheels in harmony. What the *padre* really thought of the trip is not known, but there was no doubt about his having the attention and respect of his somewhat reckless flock on Iris return to harbour. "E 4" was the sort of boat to take a passage in if one wished to see life in the Bight thoroughly.

On one occasion she rose to the surface and chased a U-boat up to Heligoland, endeavouring to instil into her opponent a spirit of pugnacity by continual signals on the arc-lamp, such as, "How many women and children have you killed today?" and in a sort of meet-you-half-way tone, "*Gott strafe* England!" The U-boat, however, was not playing, and used her superior speed to get away (which was perhaps as well, because, if she'd only known it, "E 4" at the time, had no gun).

This was early in the war, when things had not settled down and the minefields in the Bight were few. More than one boat then had dived right up to the entrance of Schillig Roads and had looked longingly at the guardship lying just out of range across the shoals. E boats treated destroyers with contempt, and used to remain on the surface in their presence to the last possible moment. There are many rumours of strange incidents of 1914 and 1915 which did not reach despatches, such as wireless signals to Heligoland suggesting that the enemy ships should come out and give our boats a chance, or of boats firing a succession of different coloured lights off the mouth of the Ems in the hope of enticing some-thing out to see what it was all about. If the wireless story is not true it is at any rate a sound idea.

We did not produce any propaganda department till much later, or they might have developed it, for such signals would have been very suggestive when intercepted by neutral wireless stations. The state of defence of the Bight changed from 1914, when our boats played about in it as they pleased, and even cruisers could come in and actually sight Heligoland, to the

1915 stage, when boats had to work inside, diving all day in the midst of enemy patrol vessels and getting their batteries charged in the intervals between alarms at night. Then the minefields began to thicken, and the submarine patrol line was brought gradually back to the longitude of Borkum. Then our minefields began to cluster around those the enemy had laid, and the patrols eventually took up a curved line from Terschelling across the mouth of the Bight to Hiorn's Reef and the Vyl Light, and remained there, except for occasional examination trips up to the enemy harbours and for the frequent visits of our minelaying submarines (which used to drop their cargoes wherever they were most likely to have full effect).

This moving back of the patrol line was not due to the increase of the Bight minefields alone: the realisation of the use of the submarine as a scout and the recognition of the fact that for our fleet the wireless in the submarines was of more strategic use than were the torpedoes, altered the policy by which the boats were stationed. A tactical victory may be useful, but it is a stategical victory that wins a war, and this fact was at the base of our policy at sea. The enemy seems never to have understood what sea-strategy meant, although his tactics were sound enough. It is a curious thing to note how the role of the submarine changed during the war. The boats of both sides started by being ordinary anti-warship craft, taking a chance when they could. Gradually our boats became outer-line scouts (with exceptions), and the U-boats (with exceptions) became exclusively commerce-destroyers.

At present anti-submarine work has advanced so far that it would be a rash nation which would endeavour to obtain a victory over another by a submarine force alone. The big cruiser-submarine is a danger, but it can be met and defeated by a better (though not necessarily bigger) submarine, while the anti-submarine work by surface ships will always be the prerogative of the nation with the big fleet in support. The submarine, as we know it now, can never win a war without a battle fleet behind it: the two types of weapon work together, and the one cannot supplant the other.

A curious remark has been made by a German officer to an English one. "If we had beaten your Fleet, you could have still kept up the blockade with your submarines, because England geographically blockades Germany, and so we would have been no better off." Geographically he was right—strategically he was, in the author's opinion, very much wrong.

The "crash dives," so frequently performed by boats when in danger, were some-times exciting. If the trim was too heavy at the time, the boat might take an angle and go right on down to the bottom: this has been done sufficiently violently at times to crack some of the battery cells, and also to start the torpedoes running in the tubes with resultant damage to the torpedoes and a discharge of exhaust gas into the boat. It is always advisable for the officer on deck to get down as soon as possible after he has rung the diving alarm-horn—otherwise he may get left behind, as the crew below don't wait for him.

The lower door of the conning-tower is dropped by an officer below if water comes down, isolating the officer in the conning-tower, who is probably struggling to get the upper lid closed. One boat had a little difficulty once through a corner of the bridge-screen catching under the hinges of the upper lid; the boat was going under—the captain was furiously trying to jam the lid down—and the water was pouring into the boat.

The captain called down to close the lower door and that he would "swim for it," but before this was done the obstruction cleared, the hatch closed, and he fell down into the boat. The depth being then thirty feet, it can be imagined that a good deal of water had come in and things had been exciting, to say the least of it; it was noticed, however, that the seamen's cook had never throughout the incident looked up once from his careful watch on the cooking of the sailors' sausages.

Another incident occurred near Heligoland, when one officer of an E boat came on deck to relieve another during the nightly three hours' charge. As he came up he saw a faint light astern and called attention to it. The officer already on deck (hereinafter known as Number One) had just passed the word down to let some more water into the tanks "till I tell you to stop," in order to lower the boat a little and leave only her conning-tower visible.

His attention being distracted to the light astern (which was on the south end of Heligoland), he began to study it with his glasses, and had dropped the memory of flooding tanks from his mind—until a shout from officer Number Two made him turn. The water was up to the tip of the conning-tower lid. The look-out and Number Two had leaped below, and the third officer, inside the boat, had his hand on the lever of the lower door and his eyes on a depth gauge, which already showed ten feet.

Number One got down inside in remarkably quick time (at the cost of some abrasions) and pulled the upper lid down after him as the North Sea came over the top. Packed in the conning-tower with him were the look-out and Number Two—both of them helpless with laughter. The third officer then blew tanks, and as the boat reached the surface again, opened the lower door and inquired if there was anybody to go back for? Fortunately there was not.

A patrol boat's crew being trained to dive quickly and to ask questions afterwards, a boat on passage with low buoyancy is rather a touchy platform to stand on. The diving alarm button is fitted just inside the conning-tower lid, and one stoops down to ring it. One officer thought that a "wandering" lead extension with a bell-push button on it would be a convenient fitting, as he could then stand on watch on the bridge and ring the alarm with his hand in his lammy-coat pocket. It worked all right till a sea came over his head and put two inches of salt water in the pocket; the bell push was not watertight, and, well, he only just got in and joined his crew before they were right under.

An E boat was once running past the Maas Lightship off the Dutch coast. She was trimmed a bit more than half down, and was travelling at fourteen knots, with a little "rise" helm on the hydroplanes. The captain and lookout were on the bridge—it was flat calm and fairly clear weather. Down below an enthusiastic stoker chose the moment as suitable for oiling-over the shafting of the after hydroplanes; he started by releasing the locking gear, and running the planes "hard-up." The boat instantly tried to loop the loop. Her bow rose till she was at an extraordinary angle—the engines slowed up and hammered violently—the look-out vanished below, the captain jumped down the ladder, rang the telegraphs to "slow," and (having realised what had happened), remained with his head and shoulders out, looking at the foaming wave of water that had risen to half-way along the bridge.

He knew that as soon as the boat slowed she would regain her normal angle, and he intended then to show that he, at any rate, was abreast of the situation, and to descend with dignity when the headway was lost, and to sarcastically liken his crew to a collection of Armenian schoolgirls. The crew, however, unwittingly defeated him. The motto of a patrol boat is, *When in doubt—dive*, and they were well-trained men. They did not know what had happened beyond that the boat had done something funny and that there was a lot of violent language going on inside her.

The captain watched the stern wave—instead of receding as the angle lessened—break right over his head, and he had to shut down quickly and come below, being met by the complacent report of "Thirty feet, sir, going down." The passing Dutch trawlers had a good view of the incident, and must have thought the boat had gone mad.

There were always so many fishing trawlers about on the Dutch coast that it was impossible for our boats to avoid being seen and noted when on passage on the surface. If possible, one gave them a wide berth in case of accidents, but none of them were ever found to be Germans in disguise. The British patrol boats were more unpleasant: an R boat nearly met her end from one off the Irish coast once at night.

The submarine was an anti-submarine patrol, and was charging on the surface, when the trawler approached and endeavoured to ram. The attempt was dodged by a matter of feet, and apparently the trawler's men were too excited to recognise the volley of verbal vitriol (that was addressed to them as they shot past) as being English, for as the R boat dropped across their stern they opened rapid fire on her with the after gun. The submarine men could look into the gun-muzzle at a few yards' range, but in spite of their being nearly deafened by a very rapid and continuous fire, there was no damage done except for a graze on the after superstructure. The submarine then used her superior speed and van shed.

Our mine-laying submarines were few in number, for the reason that we had not the need for such boats that the enemy had. We could have built more if we had wished to, but owing to the short length of enemy coastline we found that a few boats running regularly could cover the work. The mines were laid down anywhere in the Bight where results might be expected from them, and off Zeebrugge and places on the Belgian coast where enemy ships passed. There was far more secrecy over the work of mine-laying boats than that of the patrol boats, for the enemy knew quite well that we had a patrol ring round the Bight, and he probably knew roughly the number and positions of the boats we had out at any time.

But the mine-layers used to get short notice of their leaving: they hoisted their mines aboard, got their orders, and vanished to the north-eastward before anyone else in the depot had had time to wonder where they were going. A patrol boat used to have an area about ten miles by ten to work in; a mine-layer had to put the cargo absolutely on the spot ordered,—an error in navigation might mean not only that the enemy would not hit the mines, but that an E boat might run into them later under the impression that she was skirting the field.

It was customary, therefore, for the run from Harwich to be made to some light-vessel or a fixed point on the Dutch coast before entering the Bight, and for the greatest care to be taken by star observations, etc., on the run-in to check the reckoning. After the Armistice the evidence of the enemy showed that the navigation and placing of mines had been extraordinarily accurate. Two of the boats were lost on this duty, both in the Bight, and both probably through striking mines—"E 24" and "E 34."

In July 1917 "E 41" (Lieutenant-Commander Holbrook, V.C.) having just laid her mines in a swept channel in the Bight, sighted a German merchant ship approaching, guarded by an escort of patrol craft. "E 41" torpedoed the ship, and was promptly chased by the escort. She led the chase towards the spot where she had just put her mines down, and went deep herself as she crossed the dangerous area. The patrol craft, however, broke off the pursuit before they reached the spot, and turned home. A little more ardour on their part and "E 41" could have watched her own mines at work.

One mine-layer had the good fortune to pick up the laden boats of a neutral steamer which had been sunk by the enemy. She towed them into safety (her captain nobly refusing a present of a box of cigars offered him by the survivors). On his return to Harwich the officers of his flotilla rose to the occasion and presented him with a large pair of binoculars, complete in a lacquered case.

The binoculars (suitably inscribed) were formed of two beer bottles joined together, and the case was neatly made of biscuit-box tin. Suitable speeches being made and the glasses handed over, the recipient was requested to sign a "receipt note" for them. Wondering at such meticulous red-tape, he complied, and the carbon paper being removed and the under-lying "chit" sent to the wardroom steward, he discovered that his signature was the authority for drinks all round to the deputation, which, after all, was the main object for which the ceremony had been inaugurated.

CHAPTER 7

Towards the Armistice

When the Armistice came the enemy was told to notify us of the position and details of his swept channels; this he did, and it was found that there was not much in the report that was news to us. When the U-boats left Germany on their last voyage to our coast in November 1918, they came by the swept channel that runs west from Heligoland to the N. Dogger Bank Lightship; the same channel was used for the voyage of the Armistice Commission in H.M.S. *Hercules* towards Wilhelmshaven in December. It was then found that our charts were, if anything, slightly more up to date than were those of the German pilots. A despatch describing a mine-laying submarine's trip will explain why we were so fully abreast of navigational matters inside the Bight.

'E 45' (Lieutenant-Commander Gaimes).
April 22nd: Proceeded *via* X. 1 channel, Terschelling and South Dogger Bank Lightships.

April 23rd: Observed noon position 54° 30' N., 3° 53' E. 7 p.m.: Picked up first of enemy swept channel buoys and proceeded up channel.

At each buoy she passed, "E 45" fixed position and plotted her run on the chart. At 10 p.m. she dived to pass under one of our mine-groups, and at 11.30 p.m. she rose and proceeded on the surface. At 1 a.m. she went to the bottom in 99 feet till 8.15 p.m., noting in her log that the greatest rise and fall of tide shown on her depth-gauge was 4½ feet.

8.44 p.m.: Observed vessel showing white light. Dived. Continued diving through minefield.

11 p.m.: Surface. Proceeded to mine-laying position.

She then laid her mines and came away by the same route. The laying position was between Heligoland and Ruter Gat, within sight of the German examination steamer and close to the entrance in the boom defence between Heligoland and the shore. If "E 45" had been caught in the act she would have found it awkward, as there was barely enough water there for her to dive, though it was in the main entrance to the enemy local defences.

I have mentioned the case of "E 13," and described her shelling by the enemy when she lay aground on the Island of Saltholm. Of the survivors, two were at once sent to hospital, and the remainder were berthed aboard the Danish ship *Peder Skram*, all being treated with great kindness. The *Peder Skram* took them to Copenhagen and transferred them to the naval barracks. Commander Layton at once began to think of escape, and, after three weeks in Copenhagen, withdrew his parole—due notice being given on his part and precautions taken on the part of the Danes.

He knew that his only chance of escape was to so arrange matters that his absence should be undiscovered till he had time to cross the frontier to Sweden; this was done by the time-honoured method of leaving a dummy figure in his bed. He had to pass six sentries on his way out in addition to the one outside his door, but he had the assistance of his officers in this difficulty. Lieutenant Eddis distracted the door-sentry's attention while his captain crossed to Lieutenant Garriock's room, and then turned his attention to the two guard officers downstairs.

Commander Layton changed in Lieutenant Garriock's room into a suit of "acquired" Danish sailor's clothes, and left by the window down a "hammock lashing." He walked through the kitchen and pantry of the officers' block, went through the pantry window (having already arranged for "distractions" for the outside sentries), and walked off towards the jetty He passed the old mast crane (that is shown in pictures of the battle of Copenhagen, and which still looks out over waters that have seen wars innumerable), and hurried on to where the dockyard wall joins the sea.

There he took to the water and swam some way along the shore till he landed under the lock bridge at the basin entrance. He was now in the town area; he took off his clothes, wrung them out and replaced them (there was 18° of frost), then walked to the Kristiansund-Copenhagen ferry pier. He boarded the ferry and made the passage amidst a crowd of Danish sailors and police, went to a rendezvous with a friend on arrival, changed his clothes, and became a Norwegian merchant-ship mate of Finnish birth and language (Finnish interpreters are generally scarce). He then caught the first train out to Christiania, called at the Legation for a passport, and went straight on to Bergen, changing his personality on the way to that of "George Perkins, U.S.A.—a Marine Overseer."

At Bergen he boarded the Norwegian mail-boat for Newcastle, still posing as an American. His histrionic abilities, however, were rather discredited on the journey, as several fellow-passengers doubted that he really came from the States, and one tactlessly stated that he would have put him down as a British naval officer, "if he hadn't been told he was an American." At Newcastle he had considerable difficulty in establishing his identity—the sleuth instinct of a Boy Scout causing him some trouble—but he eventually cleared his character, and reached London on Tuesday, having broken out of prison at 7.30.p.m. the previous Friday.

The hue-and-cry started too late to catch him, and, partly perhaps owing to Danish sympathy with this country, and also certainly owing to his personality having become popular with the Copenhagen people during his parole period, the chase was guided by the Danish newspapers into several wrong directions.

On the 15th April 1915, Submarine "E 15" (Lieutenant-Commander T. S. Brodie) made the first attempt to enter the Sea of Marmora. She entered the Dardanelles at 2 a.m., dived at 4, and at 6.45 a.m. she struck the shore under the Turkish guns. The captain ordered all tanks to be blown, and under a terrific fire he tried to get the boat off by going full astern (she had bounced up the beach till her conning-tower and hull were exposed), and the survivors reported that he had just inquired if the hull was badly hit or not when a large shell passed through the conning-tower, killing him instantly.

Orders were given to abandon the ship, and Lieutenants Price and Fitzgerald proceeded, while shell after shell struck the boat, to destroy the charts and papers. This boat was later further demolished by a gallant British picket-boat attack. A fortnight later A E 2 was sent up, and, as has been told, was lost in the Marmora. The third and fourth boats, "E 11" and "E 14" got through safely. It is interesting to read in a German publication that the German Admiral on the spot stated later—

> The English submarines in the Marmora performed magnificently. . . . The English submarine design is excellent.

A German officer would not agree with the latter part of the remark, as every nation has a different type of boat, but certainly in the Marmora our submarine officers preferred the E type of boat to anything else.

One thing that this war has shown us is that the Germans have not got a monopoly in the manufacture of first-class optical lenses. In 1914 the German periscope was a lot better than ours; in 1915 we put out contracts for periscopes to new firms in this country; in 1916 our new periscopes equalled those of the enemy; in 1918 our latest periscopes were the best in the world.

This advance was accomplished by our firms in face of two handicaps—one, that our periscopes ordered were some seven feet longer than the enemy's; the other, that ours were to be practically vibrationless. The results gained have broken the bubble of reputation previously raised by the Jena glass factories. In the Diesel oil-engine the Germans probably lead us—in steam turbines we lead them. In general submarine design and practice we are a long way ahead, while in certain minor details they give us points to copy. Among a mass of clumsy fittings in their boats (fittings which had long ago been eliminated or simplified with us) one finds small labour-saving "gadgets" installed which we have either not thought of, or have neglected to supply.

A typically German piece of thoroughness is to be seen—one specimen on Zeebrugge Mole, the other at Wilhelmshaven. This is a raised plat-form carrying a gun on top; the platform works on eccentric bearings which are able, through the use of a separate motor, to roll or pitch the gun to a variable amount while the submarine gunlayer under training endeavours to carry out practice at a target towed past him out at sea.

It is also rereported that this arrangement is sometimes used to cure submarine sailors of excessive sea-sickness: this is probably true, as an hour's stay on the rocking platform would cure the most hardened case. As our boats did not use the gun much, such a contrivance was not needed; but in any case such shore training, as opposed to practice at sea, is against the usual habit of our Navy. Which method is right—well, there's some-thing to be said for both sides.

Early in the war the U-boats were faster than the E's by quite two knots. Later our patrol boats became two knots faster than the later U's, while, of course, our Fleet submarines were much faster still. In gun-power the U-boats were always better, because they wanted guns more for their work. This implied that our boats were always the faster under water. In speed of diving, i.e. in time of getting under, there was practically no difference between the two types.

In endurance the types were, ton for ton, the same, though our boats were probably far more comfortable and roomy to live in. In torpedo armament (i.e. in number of tubes) there was no comparison—our boats were always the more heavily armed. In wireless installations we were behindhand in 1914-15, but were ahead in 1918. In general steadiness of diving and control and in under-water handling we were always ahead. In structural strength and capacity to resist the pressures of great depths of water the enemy were probably slightly better. In hydroplane installations the American boats seem to be ahead of both of us. Neither the

English nor German boats recorded a success due to the use of hydrophones, and they appear to have been little used by either Submarine Service. Both, however, used the under-water sound-signalling gear (of Fessenden type) with success, and it was found to be a useful adjunct to submarine work. Each Navy was fitting larger torpedoes and warheads in 1918 in view of the fact that the modern surface war-ship was found to be difficult to sink with the usual eighteen-inch weapon.

It will be gathered from the above that we had and still have a lead in design and construction. What is far more important, however, is the lead we have kept in training and quality of the officers and men. The Germans improvised a Submarine Service—we had one already before the war, and we simply expanded it "according to plan," as more boats were needed.

On the outbreak of war, the Submarine Service, as did the surface fleet, added to its personnel by the use of Royal Naval Reserve officers, and "hostilities only" ratings, the latter being usually men with experience as motor mechanics or workshop engineers. These ratings were employed either in the depot ship workshops or in the engine-rooms of sea-going submarines, and they there justified their presence by the sound and keen work they performed under strange and often dangerous circumstances.

The R.N.R. officers were used as watch-keepers and navigators in the boats, and their history in the war is shown in their long list of decorations and casualties. They were not expected to learn much of the technicalities of submarines—there were other officers aboard who could look after that side of the business—but in many cases they taught themselves far more than had been expected, with the result that they were able to substitute on occasions the regularly trained officers. Their chief duty, however, lay in watch-keeping and navigating: nothing could approach the air of calm detachment with which an R.N.R. would go forward to his bunk to turn in, after he had—halfway through his nightwatch on deck—pressed the button of the diving alarm at sight of an enemy patrol boat close aboard, closed the lid, descended with a rush, and reported the cause of the alarm to the captain.

By the time the captain had checked the descent and levelled the boat at sixty feet, the R.N.R. lieutenant would be snoring peacefully, the matter being out of his head once he had taken his decision to give the "crash-dive" order. All through the war we carried an R.N.R. officer aboard every sea-going submarine as a "third-hand," and the Service owes a very great deal to the help of these competent and loyal auxiliaries.

The following is written of a combination of two or more true war incidents. It is intended to illustrate what the writer considers to be the true strategic use of patrol submarines.

After 1916 the Submarine Patrol flotillas that watched the exit of the Heligoland Bight were given certain orders, which altered altogether their duties and their *raison d'être*. These were to the effect that no outward-bound ship of the enemy was to be attacked or fired at until a signal had first been made by the sighting submarine, to report such enemy's presence and movement; only homeward-bound ships could be fired at, and if outward-bound ships were seen, the reporting signal was to be made at all costs.

This alteration detracted somewhat from the interest of submarine war, but it added largely to the strategic usefulness of our patrol boats. It is of no use to torpedo an enemy ship and thereby lose a chance for the Grand Fleet of cutting off the whole enemy force, and a torpedo fired meant that an hour or more of depth-charging would follow the shot, and prevent the signal being made before the news of the enemy's position had grown cold.

The submarine was a J boat, and her station was at the western end of the North Dogger Bank-Heligoland swept channel. The weather had been rough and wet for the first four days of her patrol, reducing the periscope visibility to a few hundred yards' range across grey and foaming seas. The boat had patrolled at twenty feet depth (which is shallow for a big boat) in order to see anything at all, and because of the steep seas she had kept always beam to them, except for the turns at the end of her ten-mile beat. Each turn had caused her to either break surface or slip down to eighty feet, owing to the quick inclinations given her as the waves met her end-on.

The weather cleared suddenly on the fourth night, and next morning she dived at dawn, under a gentle swell that hourly died down to a calm deep blue ocean. The visibility was good—how good her captain had hardly realised until through his high-power periscope he picked up the unmistakable line of brown blurs to the east that meant an approaching enemy squadron at a range of at least ten miles He turned and dived at half-speed towards them, calling his crew to "action stations" at once. He knew that his orders forbade him to fire, but there was always the chance of his having to use his torpedoes in self-defence—self-defence, that is, of a legitimate kind, not of the type said to be used in certain districts where only mad elephants are allowed to be killed, but where all the elephants are said to became indubitably mad "after the first shot."

As the smoke-blurs grew he eased speed to "dead slow"; the enemy was shown by the rate of change of his bearings to be steering a course which would take him past the J boat at easy range. The periscope slid along very slowly, only about a foot of its length showing above water; the captain knew that he could see Zeppelins if they were about, but an aeroplane, especially against the sun, is a different proposition, and he did not want to risk being observed before his wireless had done its work. Twenty minutes from sighting the smoke he turned to east to pass parallel to the enemy, and he moved slowly past their line.

Looking closely at them with the high-power instrument, and with his periscope top now a bold three feet above the surface, he spoke rapidly and briefly to his third officer, who, notebook in hand, stood at his elbow—

....Four light cruisers—*Pillau, Königsberg,* and two more—line ahead two cables—speed twenty—course west. A destroyer screen on each bow—two aside. Away to starboard of them at five miles are five battle-cruisers—the usual lot with a big screen—too smoky to count. Cut that down, make a signal of it and get it coded, quick!

He trained the periscope to eastward again, stared for a minute at the horizon, and then lowered the big instrument down into its well. There was apparently nothing following the two squadrons, and he intended to rise and snap in his wireless signal as soon as they had left him far enough astern—say seven miles—to make it fairly safe for him to do so. After ten minutes he raised his periscope for a look, then lowered it and studied his watch for ten minutes more. Another searching sweep of the horizon and—"Stand by for surface—Smack that signal off the moment the aerial's up, Pilot—all ready there? Surface...."

The lid swung open as the top of the hull showed, and the captain nipped straight up on to the bridge rail and looked astern towards the haze of brown smoke that marked where the German battle-cruisers were steaming on. After one glance he twisted round to look forward and raised his glasses; lowering them, he gave a general look round and overhead, then beckoned to the messenger (a seaman who stood in the conning-tower with his head just below the lid of the hatch)."Tell the first lieutenant to stop blowing and to come up...."

Twenty seconds later his subordinate was beside him, and he spoke over his shoulder, watching the horizon to the east. "More of 'em coming out—tell the operator to get a hustle on—I'll have to dip in five minutes or they'll see us."

The first lieutenant nodded and turned to jump down the ladder. "Zeppelin to starboard," he said as he vanished; "long way up."

The captain nodded—glanced at the distant airship, and

continued his watch on the approaching ships. He had a mild contempt both for a Zeppelin's offensive powers and for her capability of seeing submarine conning-towers at anything but short range. In any case, she was five minutes' flight away at least, and he hoped to be under water again by that time. The enemy squadron appeared at long range to be composed of four more light cruisers with no destroyer screen, and steaming in either quarter-line or line abreast—a formation perhaps adopted as a precaution against submarine attack. After three minutes he began to tap his hand impatiently against the periscope standard; after five, he stepped down and looked anxiously down the conning-tower. The first lieutenant was just coming up the ladder.

"Well?"

"He's burnt out a coil, sir, and it'll take a few minutes; signal's not started yet."

The captain swore shortly; then—"Open up engines."

The captain watched the first lieutenant's cap vanish below, then turned to watch the approaching enemy. He was going to cut it rather fine, and the knowledge of the chances he was taking removed his impatience and anxiety. Now that he had made up his mind he felt quite cheerful again. If luck was against him he might get sunk, but the enemy's chance of damaging him in five minutes was small.

As he raised his glasses he saw the dull red flash he had been expecting break out from the bows of three of the four cruisers, followed a couple of seconds later by the flame of the fourth. Each cruiser was hidden a moment in a brown ball of smoke, which dissipated before she had passed through it. Through his glasses he saw, high up over their mastheads, a group of little black dots that rose and grew larger; the dots seemed to swerve a little to the left in their flight, as a low-sliced cleek-shot would do, then they slowly descended towards him.

When they were some ten degrees above the horizon he lost sight of them, and at the instant the water, four hundred yards short of the J boat, leaped up in fifty-foot spouts to the sound of great cart-whips cracking. A big lump of broken shell passed over with a rhythmical whine and stutter—a lump obviously of bad stream-line shape for flying at high speed. The fourth shell pitched a long way short, failed to burst, and came over in a high ricochet, making a noise like a goods train passing. The J boat's helm went over, and she steered for the white mist that still hung where the first shells fell.

As she steadied on her course the water under her bows— fifty yards off—turned white, and leaped up in a high solid pillar to the impact of the next salvo. Her helm went hard over, but too late to avoid her bath; she passed through the edge of the water-spout and took the full rain of it over her bridge and conning-tower. The first lieutenant arrived on deck in time to receive a full douche of spray, and to see, a moment later, the fourth ship's erratic contribution fall explosively two hundred yards on the bow and short again. He wiped the water from his face with the sodden sleeve of his sweater and spoke quickly: "Signal's passing now, sir. Shall he wait for an acknowledgment?"

"No, make it twice and stand by to dip. We can stand another salvo or two. . . ."

"Are they only using bow guns?"

"Yes; if they turn and fire all guns it won't be safe. They'll be astern next salvo. . . ."

The first lieutenant had vanished again—the boat had spun round (on the principle of steering for the last general splash, and trusting to the meticulous routine of German gunnery corrections) when, with a vicious crack, the three shells passed over the bridge and burst on the water close aboard beyond the hull. The captain ducked—not so much from surprise, but to avoid what he knew was coming; he looked down the conning-tower and saw the third officer's mouth frame the words, "Signal passed"; he jumped down, pressing the diving alarm with one hand as he reached up with the other to close the lid.

Then number four shell came, falling a few yards short of his saddle tanks, and sending a shower of water and small splinters across the boat: as usually happens, the bad shot had come near-est, though splinters are not of much use against a submarine

155

hull. The lid snapped down and the tail kicked up a little, and a ragged salvo of shell from the broad-sides of four light cruisers whitened the sea where the target had been. The ships turned again and started on a wide sweep round the spot before edging back to their leader's course. (No ship unattended by destroyers will risk approaching the place where a submarine has dived.) Up the ladder to the leader's bridge ten miles ahead a messenger ran, and stood panting as he held out a signal from the wireless office for the Rear-Admiral to read. The Admiral nodded and looked astern—"No doubt of its origin," he said, frowning. "They call that their Submarine Emergency Reporting Code. We shall alter course."

The fight between the submarine and its enemies has been waged throughout the war with great intensity of feeling. The sub-marine weapon aroused hatred aboard surface ships just because it made them feel helpless (I am not referring to acts outside the pale of International or Human laws). The submarine felt—well, not hatred, but fear. There is a ruthlessness of action which is apparently born of cruelty, but which is really due to instincts of self-preservation alone.

When "U 18" torpedoed and sank "E 22," she rose, in spite of the danger of attack by other E boats near, and picked up the survivors; she could, in view of the fact that her enemies were three miles off, risk doing this. Our own boats have on practically every occasion picked up the survivors of the U-boats they have sunk,—this because, having command of the sea, we could be sure in local waters of nothing hostile interfering.

When Lieutenant D'Oyley-Hughes, however, sank "U 153" off Cape St Vincent, and rose to pick up the men in the water, he saw another U-boat dive at him from close quarters, which forced him to go under also. In consequence the survivors were drowned—a contingency which might have been avoided if the two belligerent submarines diving round the spot could have trusted each other sufficiently to rise with a white flag flying.

As things were, neither would risk being torpedoed on the surface. This spirit was induced early in the war (the incidents which started the feeling need not be quoted), and it is regretted that there was throughout no International arrangement by which a submarine could "go out of play" for a while with a white flag hoisted. The fact that the enemy's War-Book directly permits a breach of rules, if such breach is of vital necessity, is a great bar to the drawing up of humane and decent laws on the subject; while, of course, a breach of the rules by an angry surface vessel (no unlikely thing to occur) would at once abrogate all the rules in the minds of submarine people.

There is no doubt that a new weapon calls for new laws to control and guide its use. The enemy boats were used illegally because the enemy Government ordered such use. In certain cases the U-boat captains exceeded their instructions and acted yet more illegally. In such cases it rests with the enemy Government to repudiate or approve their subordinates' actions. In our submarine service we had no orders to be "frightful," and therefore we were humane and acted legally; if we had had such orders as the enemy gave, we would have carried them out, and, from a technical point of view, carried them out much better.

But we would have had no instances of personal excess in such acts, just because that sort of thing would not have appealed to our officers. I should mention that the cases of "excess" among U-boat captains were confined to a few, in comparison with the numbers employed, and certain of those few met their deaths before they could return to tell of their deeds. If submarines are allowed to navies of the future, they must have a code of rules to work by. The code should be drawn up by people who know their subject, and who are also influenced in their ideas by the laws of chivalry and not by the ideas of the German War-Book. Apart from questions of right or wrong, unnecessary killing in war does not pay.

Anybody can think of instances of this, but to suggest a case: if a U-boat had been sunk by our patrol vessels while she was in the act of picking up survivors from a torpedoed ship, well, the Germans would have lost a U-boat, but would have gained a splendid piece of propaganda. The patrol vessels could not be blamed, but the U-boat Service would have had a good grievance for the rest of the war. It is not only what you do in war that counts—the way you do it has a lot of influence also on the ultimate result. It is true that war is the negation of ethics, and that expediency is the ruling motive in all war-like acts, but it is a mistake to think, as the enemy did, that ruthlessness pays—decency may very often pay better.

In war, a nation must take the blame for the acts of its militant servants; it sometimes pays to disavow such acts, and to sacrifice a subordinate, but in the main all blame must fall on the Government giving the orders. The essence of a military or naval force is discipline, and owing to that discipline all responsibility must in the end be shouldered by the Governments, except in the cases where individual officers have exceeded their orders or interpreted them to the dissatisfaction of their seniors.

In our Submarine Service no boat left harbour without definite written orders, and the exact spirit in which her duty was to be carried out was fully understood. If any officer at any time had departed from his orders to the extent of "frightfulness," he would have found himself at once in a serious position: as nobody ever tried the experiment, I cannot quote any cases.

I cannot do better, in speaking of the crews of our boats, than to quote from a despatch of Commodore Keyes (as he was then), written in 1914:—

When a submarine is submerged, her captain alone is able to see what is taking place; the success of the enterprise and the safety of the vessel depend on his skill and nerve, and the prompt, precise execution of his orders by the officers and men under his command. Our submarines have been pioneers in waters which might well have been mined. They have been subjected to skilful and well-thought-out anti-submarine tactics by a highly-trained and determined enemy, attacked by gunfire and torpedo, driven to lie on the bottom at a great depth to preserve battery-power, hunted for hours at a time by hostile torpedo craft. . . . Sudden alterations of course and depth, the sound of propellers overhead, and the concussion of bursting shells, give an indication to the crew of the risks to which they are being exposed; and it speaks well for the morale of these young officers and men, and their gallant faith in their captains, that they have invariably carried out their duties quietly, keenly, and confidently under conditions which might well have tried the most hardened veteran. The Commanding Officers of the submarines are of the opinion that it is impossible to single out individuals when all performed their duties so admirably, and in this I concur. ...

That description of the submarine sailor held good throughout the war, as in 1914.

There is another despatch of 1914, which gives a clear picture of Heligoland patrol work in the winter months:—

During the past week these submarines have experienced very heavy westerly gales ... a short steep sea which made it impossible to open the conning-tower hatch, vision limited to that obtained through the periscopes (*i.e.* only a cable or two between the seas that continually broke over them). The submarines were thus an easy prey to any surface vessel falling in with them, and it was therefore necessary to keep submerged; also, to make an offing, as there were no means of obtaining the position except by sinking to the bottom and obtaining soundings.

There was no rest on the bottom even at a depth of 22 fathoms, as the submarines were rolling and bumping there in spite of considerable negative buoyancy, and it was therefore necessary to keep under way at a depth clear of the keels of possible ships. At this depth motion was considerable, and pumping (*i.e.* vertical motion) was 20 to 30 feet. When battery-power became low, it was necessary to come to the surface, as lying on the bottom was dangerous.

On the surface, it was necessary to keep a ventilator open

to run the engines, in order to keep head to sea; through this ventilator much water was shipped. ... No good purpose can be served in maintaining the close blockade of the Bight in such weather. Even if the enemy emerged, which is unlikely, it would be almost impossible to bring off a successful attack.

I have in this history only quoted typical despatches and incidents in the work of our submarines. It would take many books to quote them all. I feel that I have dealt with a great story in an inadequate way, but only a great writer could deal with it faithfully. Trying to sum up impressions of four years of war, I find that two memories stand out and hide the rest: one is of the face of a hydroplane man as he sat leaning forward to watch his gauge—his whole attention fixed on the movement of the needle and on his own job—oblivious of the rushing sound of turbine-driven propellers as German destroyers passed overhead; the other is of the salvage of one of our boats three weeks after she sank, when we found each officer and man at his station as they had died after every detail of their drill had been carried out, and of the feeling of respect—even, perhaps, of envy of men who had passed such a test without a failure—with which one raised and carried them away.

One wanted to be able to tell them so, but I think they did know, at any rate before they died, that their fellow-craftsmen would approve, as the men of Major Wilson's patrol must have known at the Shangani River in '93, that those who came to bury them would recognise that they had died well.

The Submarine Service was good before the war. The many who have died in the boats since have given it a tradition that will ensure its standard being always maintained: such men have given the survivors a high code to live up to. I will conclude by quoting a message from the Commodore of Submarines, which was promulgated to all the boats after the Armistice:—

12th November 1918.
Now that a General Armistice is in force, I wish to lose no

time in tendering my personal tribute to the officers and men of the Submarine Service.

Having had a good deal to do with this Service in its early stages, it has been a great honour and a great pleasure to command it in war, and it must be a source of great pride and satisfaction to you, as it is to me, that our peace organisation and training have withstood the supreme test, and that you have so splendidly carried out the many and varied services demanded of you.

Submarines were the first at sea on the outbreak of war, they have been continuously in action while it lasted, they will be the last to return to harbour.

"You have, in addition to the invaluable outpost, patrol, mine-laying, fleet duties, and other services, the sinking of 54 enemy warships and 274 other vessels to your credit, and you have done more to counter the enemy's illegal war upon commerce than any other single means; at the same time you have been called upon to man new and intricate types of submarines, demanding the highest standard of knowledge and efficiency. Your steadiness and grit, whilst the toll of your gallant fellows was heavy, has been beyond all praise, and will form glorious pages in naval history when this comes to be written.

You have established a magnificent record of strenuous and gallant service, of clean fighting and devotion to duty that must always be a source of keen satisfaction to you for the rest of your lives, as it will be a great tradition to hand down to those who follow you.

It is inevitable, from the nature of submarines, that your senior officers cannot lead you into action as they would wish. It has been my duty to try and get you the best material, to maintain fairness and equity on the sole ground of personal efficiency, and to maintain your reputation for efficiency and modesty.

In this I have been so ably and loyally assisted by all without distinction, that I can never sufficiently express my gratitude and admiration for you. The result was certain. We leave the war with a record as proud as any that war has ever produced.

S. S. Hall,
Commodore (S.).